Jane S. Longuest
August, 1955

CHURCHILL
His Life in Photographs

CHURCHILL

His Life in Photographs

EDITED BY

RANDOLPH S. CHURCHILL

AND

HELMUT GERNSHEIM

RINEHART AND COMPANY, INC., ON MURRAY HILL, NEW YORK

First Published 1955

Book designed by Lewis Woudhuysen MSIA

MANUFACTURED IN GREAT BRITAIN

Foreword

The main work of selecting the four hundred pictures in which this book seeks to tell the life story of Sir Winston Churchill was undertaken by Mr Helmut Gernsheim. The final choice of photographs was based on his examination of tens of thousands. Apart from producing about thirty hitherto unpublished photographs from private sources, my task has been limited to editing the captions and letterpress.

Sir Winston must be one of the most photogenic men who ever lived. It is the rarest thing to find a really bad photograph of him. In nearly every one the likeness springs to the eye. The process of final selection was accompanied by many fierce arguments. Our object was to choose the most striking photographs covering the whole span of his life and at the same time to make sure that every important event in it was, as far as could be, recorded. We have also sought to show him with as many of his friends and contemporaries as possible.

Doubtless this collection is far from perfect, and there must be many hundreds of photographs in private hands which have never yet been published. As this book may well be reprinted, I shall be very grateful to anyone who can fill any gaps, particularly in his early life, by sending me photographs from either public or private sources.

Blenheim
1 March 1955

Randolph S. Churchill.

CHAPTER ONE

Winston Leonard Spencer-Churchill was born at Blenheim Palace, Woodstock, Oxford-shire on 30 November 1874. He was christened Winston after his ancestor, Sir Winston Churchill, the Cavalier knight who was the father of John Churchill, first Duke of Marl-borough; the name Leonard he derived from his maternal grandfather, Mr Leonard Jerome of New York. His father, Lord Randolph Churchill, the third son of the seventh Duke of Marlborough, was at that time a young Conservative member of Parliament who had made little mark upon the House. In 1876, the Duke of Marlborough was appointed Viceroy of Ireland. Lord Randolph accompanied his father to Dublin as his private secretary and took with him his wife and young child. Sir Winston has recorded in later life that it is from this period that his earliest recollections date.

'I remember', he has written, 'my grandfather, the Viceroy, unveiling the Lord Gough statue in 1878. A great black crowd, scarlet soldiers on horseback, strings pulling away a brown shiny sheet, the old Duke, the formidable grandpapa, talking loudly to the crowd. I recall even a phrase he used: "and with a withering volley he shattered the enemy's line".'

Soon after the family returned to England in 1879, the young boy was pressed into the routine educational system of the time, passing with distaste and without much profit from a series of preparatory schools to Harrow. Of this period he wrote:

'The Harrow custom of calling the roll is different from that of Eton. At Harrow they file past a Master in the schoolyard and answer one by one. My position was therefore revealed in its somewhat invidious humility. It was the year 1887. Lord Randolph Churchill had only just resigned his position as Leader of the House of Commons and Chancellor of the Exchequer, and he still towered in the forefront of politics. In consequence large num-bers of visitors of both sexes used to wait on the school steps, in order to see my march by; and I frequently heard the irreverent comment, "Why, he's last of all!" '

1874 - 1908

From Harrow he passed to Sandhurst and thence to three years with a cavalry regiment in India. It was while he was stationed there that he acquired his love of polo, a game which he was to play for the next thirty years of his life. It was here too that his intellect awakened and that by prolonged and concentrated reading he began to make good the ground he had lost during his school days. His adventurous spirit led him to the scene of most of the small wars of the period and by the time he was 23 he had seen action in three continents. Happy though he was in the Army, his ambitions were now to lead him into other fields.

After standing unsuccessfully as Conservative candidate in a by-election at Oldham in 1899 he went to South Africa to report the Boer War for the *Morning Post*. His capture by the Boers and his spectacular escape made him a world-famous figure overnight. On his return to England, he stood once more for Oldham in the 'Khaki' Election of 1900 and entered the House of Commons where, with the exception of a two year interval, he was to spend the rest of his life. When in 1904 Mr Joseph Chamberlain stampeded the Conservative Party into the policy of Tariff Reform, Mr Churchill's Free Trade convictions led him to cross the floor of the House and to join the Liberal Party. When the Liberals won their great electoral victory in 1906, he became Under-Secretary of State for the Colonies in Sir Henry Campbell-Bannerman's administration. His chief, Lord Elgin, was in the House of Lords and it fell to him to pilot through the House of Commons the Transvaal Constitution Bill, the magnanimity of which reconciled to the Empire the defeated Boers of South Africa. This was congenial to him for in his maiden speech five years before he had pleaded for a vigorous finish to the war with a humane and just settlement to follow. In 1908 he entered the Cabinet as President of the Board of Trade. This chapter closes in that year when he also, in his own words, 'married and lived happily ever afterwards'.

1 John Churchill, 1st Duke of Marlborough, (1650–1722) the victor of Blenheim and architect of the Grand Alliance against Louis XIV. Son of a poor Cavalier knight, Sir Winston Churchill, he founded the family from which the latter-day Sir Winston is sprung.

2 The 7th Duke of Marlborough (1822–1883), Sir Winston's paternal grandfather. He was Lord President of the Council and Viceroy of Ireland during Mr Disraeli's administration.

3 Leonard Jerome (1818–1891), Sir Winston's maternal grandfather. The proprietor of the *New York Times*, he has also been acclaimed as the father of the American turf.

4 Lord Randolph Churchill (1849–1895), the third son of the 7th Duke of Marlborough and the father of Sir Winston. A leading spirit in the Fourth Party in the '80s, he had a political career of exceptional brilliance, becoming at the age of 36 Leader of the House of Commons and Chancellor of the Exchequer in Lord Salisbury's Government.

5 Sir Winston's mother, Lady Randolph Churchill (1854–1921), daughter of Leonard Jerome. She was brought up in Paris and first met Lord Randolph Churchill at Cowes in August 1873. They fell in love at first sight. She was one of the great beauties of her age and Sir Winston has written of her: 'She shone for me like the evening star. I loved her dearly – but at a distance.'

6 Blenheim Palace in the Royal Borough of Woodstock in Oxfordshire. Built for John, 1st Duke of Marl-borough by the architect-playwright Vanbrugh, it was the birthplace of Sir Winston. The lake, one of the largest artificial sheets of water in England, was made by the famous landscape gardener 'Capability' Brown in the 1760s about 40 years after Blenheim had been completed. Sir Winston has described Blenheim 'as an Italian palace set in an English Park'. It was here in the early years of this century he wrote his life of his father.

7 The room in which Sir Winston was born on 30 November 1874. It is on the ground floor near the long library and was one of a suite allocated in the 1st Duke's time to his domestic chaplain, Dean Jones.

8 The earliest known portrait, aged 2, with his mother. 1876

9 Aged 6, with his aunt Lady Leslie, Lady Randolph's sister. 1880

10 Winston in a sailor's suit at the age of 7. 1881

11 Winston aged 10 with his younger brother Jack. 1884

12 Wearing a straw hat, Winston sits beside his mother at a garden party given by Sir Whittaker and Lady Ellis in Richmond. c 1886

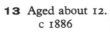

13 Aged about 12. c 1886

14 Winston, aged about 15, and Jack with their mother.
c 1889

15 Lord Randolph had been at Eton, but Winston was sent to Harrow. Its position on the hill was thought to be better for his weak lungs, a defect which has happily not been very apparent in his subsequent career. 1889

16 From Harrow, Winston went to the Royal Military Academy, Sandhurst, as a cavalry cadet. Though he had some difficulty in passing the entrance examination, he passed out eighth out of one hundred and fifty. c 1893

17 With two friends at Sandhurst just before leaving to be commissioned in the 4th Queen's Own Hussars. 1894

18 A subaltern, he wears the full dress uniform of the regiment. Now he is its honorary Colonel-in-Chief. 1895

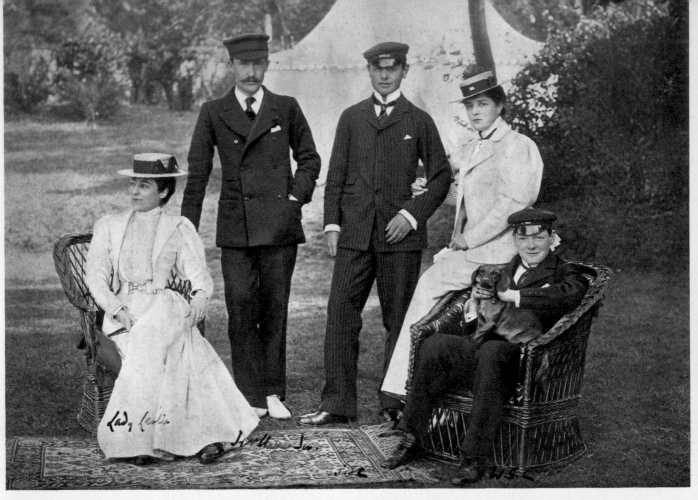

19 At the regatta at Cowes in the Isle of Wight with Lady Leslie, Mr H. V. Warrender, his brother Jack and Lady Randolph. 1895

20 Lady Randolph with her two sons, Jack and Winston; shortly afterwards Winston sailed to India with his regiment. 1896

21 The 4th Hussars were stationed at Bangalore, the military cantonment in South India, where this picture was taken. 1896

22 After seeing active service in India and commanding a troop of 21st Lancers in the charge of the Battle of Omdurman in the Sudan, Mr Churchill determined to embark on a political career. He stands as the Conservative candidate in Oldham and was defeated by 1,300 votes by Mr Walter Runciman. 1899

23 Mr Churchill's reputation as a war correspondent was already made by his books and when the Boer War broke out in South Africa, he went there as special correspondent for the *Morning Post* at £250 a month. 1899

24 In South Africa, he accompanies an armoured train which was to assist the cavalry. The train is shelled and the trucks derailed. 1899

25 Though a civilian, Mr Churchill took charge and managed to extricate most of the train. He himself became a prisoner-of-war. 1899

26 Within a month, Mr Churchill escaped from his prison camp. After a long and adventurous trip across country he arrived at Durban via Portuguese East Africa. In Durban he is greeted with bands and flags and addresses the crowd in front of the Town Hall. December 1899

27 After taking part in the action for the relief of Ladysmith and the capture of Johannesburg and Pretoria, Mr Churchill returned to England. In the 'Khaki' Election of 1900 he turned the tables on Mr Runciman at Oldham and was returned to Parliament. 1900

28 During the summer of 1901 he spent a holiday in Scotland at Guisachin, the home of Lord Tweedmouth. In the trap are Sir Edward Grey, the future Foreign Secretary, and his wife. Mr Haldane stands by the wheel. Lord Tweedmouth holds the horse. 1901

29 Smoking in the conservatory with Lord Portsmouth and Mr Haldane, later Liberal Secretary of State for War. 1901

30 On a picnic with Lady Grey, Lord Portsmouth and Mr Haldane. Behind Mr Churchill is Lady Glynn. 1901

31 Damming a Scottish burn. Mr Churchill walks across the dam to join Lady Glynn and Mr Haldane. 1901

32 With his cousin Lord Tweedmouth, he is in difficulty with a motor car.
1901

33 At Blenheim with the young American Duchess of Marlborough, formerly Miss Consuelo Vanderbilt. She is now Madame Balsan. 1901

34 A portrait taken at the time that he left the Conservatives and joined the Liberal Party. 1904

35 In camp with the Oxfordshire and Buckinghamshire Hussars, Mr Churchill is incorrectly and unconventionally dressed. He wears his familiar black and white spotted bow tie with his South African campaigning hat. On his right is his brother and squatting, his cousin, the late Duke of Marlborough.

36 In 1908 he was appointed President of the Board of Trade and entered the Cabinet at the age of 33. In those days 'on accepting an office of profit under the Crown', Members of Parliament had to seek re-election. He addresses a crowd in North West Manchester where he was defeated. A few weeks later he was elected for Dundee and represented that seat in Parliament until the fall of the Coalition in 1922. 24 April 1908

37 Arriving at Downing Street with his friend and Cabinet colleague, Mr John Morley, Secretary of State for India. 7 July 1908

38 In 1908 he became engaged to Miss Clementine Hosier. This is the first known picture of them together. 1908

39 He arrives at Caxton Hall to obtain his marriage licence. September 1908

40 At St Margaret's Church on his wedding day with his best man, Lord Hugh Cecil, now Lord Quickswood. 12 September 1908

41 After the wedding, Mrs Churchill in her going-away dress leaves the house of her aunt, Lady St Helier. 12 September 1908

CHAPTER TWO

This chapter covers a period of 13 years. No other equal period of Mr Churchill's life was crowded with so many and so varied political events. For the first two years, at the Board of Trade and at the Home Office, he was intimately concerned with the far-reaching social legislation which Mr Asquith's famous Government put on the Statute Book. He also played a leading part in defending Mr Lloyd George's Budget of 1909, in the passage of the Parliament Act which notably reduced the powers of the House of Lords and in the historic fight between the Liberal and Tory Parties about the future of Ireland.

In 1911 Mr Asquith, alarmed by German naval expansion, asked Mr Churchill to change places with Mr Reginald McKenna. Mr Asquith had offered Mr Churchill the Admiralty two years before, but he had preferred to go to the Home Office. At that time he was opposed to rearmament. But when he went to the Admiralty, he was as apprehensive of the German menace as Mr Asquith and the Foreign Secretary, Sir Edward Grey. He at once began an expanded programme of ship-building and brought all Britain's immense naval establishments to the highest state of efficiency. When war came in 1914, the Royal Navy was at its peak and within a few months all German warships and raiders had been swept from the seas. Britain continued to maintain complete control of the seas until two years later when the arrival of the U-Boat in much larger numbers threatened her with starvation.

At the opening of 1915, both the Allied and the German armies were bogged down in France and Flanders. From the Alps to the sea a double line of trenches, barbed wire, fortifications and mud had reduced the war to a stalemate.

While at the Admiralty, Mr Churchill had two conceptions for breaking the deadlock. One was the idea of the tank of which he ordered the first prototypes when he was still First Lord, and the other was the idea of turning the enemy's flank by forcing the Dardanelles. This latter enterprise foundered on miscalculation and mismanagement. To-day, however, most military historians consider that the strategical conception was sound and that with proper military organisation the enterprise would have succeeded and would have greatly shortened the war. The ruin of the Dardanelles lead to Mr Churchill's dismissal from the Admiralty. After a few months as Chancellor of the Duchy of Lancaster, he left the Government and joined the Army in France. There, after a period of instruction in trench warfare with the Grenadier Guards, he was given command of a battalion of the Royal Scots Fusiliers.

Meanwhile, Mr Lloyd George had replaced Mr Asquith as Prime Minister. He was anxious to include Mr Churchill in his Government but the Opposition still held him responsible for everything that had gone wrong in the Dardanelles. Eventually Mr Lloyd George had his way and Mr Churchill rejoined the Government in 1917 as Minister of Munitions. Here he was able largely to increase the flow of war supplies, notably of aircraft and of the tanks for which, as we have seen, he had ordered the prototypes some years earlier. Shortly after the Armistice in 1918 he was appointed Secretary of State for War and he had the difficult job of demobilising the enormous armies which Britain had sent overseas. This work completed, he became Colonial Secretary and in that capacity presided over the famous Cairo Conference in 1922 which established peace and security in the Middle East on solid foundations which survived until the outbreak of the Second World War.

The chapter ends with the fall of the Coalition Government, the victory of the Tories under Mr Bonar Law, and Mr Churchill's own defeat at Dundee which he had represented for 16 years. In the last photograph but one of this chapter will be seen a figure who will soon be familiar in these pages, Mr Churchill's detective, Sergeant Thompson of Scotland Yard. The assassination by Irish terrorists of Field Marshal Sir Henry Wilson in June 1922, led the British Government to allot bodyguards to all the British signatories of the Irish Treaty. Henceforward, Sergeant (later Inspector) Thompson is Mr Churchill's shadow.

42 Driving past the Reform Club in King's Street, Manchester. Beside him is Mr C. P. Scott, the famous proprietor of the *Manchester Guardian*, and Mr W. E. Thompson. Mr Churchill, now President of the Board of Trade, is smiling to a group of suffragettes. 22 May 1909

43 In order to cope with unemployment, Labour Exchanges were established where people seeking work could register. Mr and Mrs Churchill are seen leaving the first one to be opened in Whitechapel. 1 February 1910

44 Mr Churchill, now Home Secretary, walks to the House of Commons with the Chancellor of the Exchequer. Mr Lloyd George is carrying Mr Gladstone's despatch box which contains his Budget speech. Budget Day 1910

45 Leaving Buckingham Palace with his cousin, the Duke of Marlborough, after calling to pay their respects as Privy Counsellors on the death of King Edward VII. 6 May 1910

46 Shooting pheasants at Warter Priory, the home of Lord Nunburnholme. December 1910

47 With Mrs Churchill and General Bruce Hamilton during the British army manoeuvres at Aldershot. Summer 1910

48 Leaving a Cabinet meeting with the Foreign Secretary, Sir Edward Grey, and the Secretary for India, the Marquess of Crewe. 1910

49 Descending the gangway of a Channel steamer after taking leave of his sister-in-law, Lady Gwendeline Churchill, and the Prime Minister, Mr Asquith. c 1910

50, 51 A group of anarchists, who some days before had shot four police constables, were reported to be surrounded at a house in the East End of London, 100 Sydney Street. Mr Churchill, as Home Secretary, at once proceeded to the scene and took charge of the situation. The Tory leader, Mr Balfour, criticised him in the House: 'We are concerned to observe photographs in the illustrated papers of the Home Secretary in the danger zone. I understand what the photographer was doing, but why the Home Secretary?' An enquiry was subsequently held into what became known as the battle of Sydney Street and Mr Churchill gives evidence. His brother Jack, chin in hand, is seated on the right. January 1911

52 As Home Secretary, Mr Churchill was appointed an Ecclesiastical Commissioner for England. He leaves Buckingham Palace after a convocation of clergy. 2 March 1911

GRAHAME WHITE.

54 Mr and Mrs Churchill drive through Trafalgar Square at the coronation of King George V and Queen Mary. 22 June 1911

53 At an aviation rally, Mr Churchill talks with the newspaper proprietor, Lord Northcliffe. Mrs Churchill screens her eyes on the left. May 1911

55 In October 1911, Mr Churchill moved from the Home Office and leaves his new office for the first time as First Lord of the Admiralty. October 1911

56, 57 Mr and Mrs Churchill playing at the seaside with their one year old son Randolph. Summer 1912

58, 59 In a dog-cart while holidaying in Scotland. On the same occasion he reads in the sun with Lady Gwendeline Churchill and Mrs Churchill. 1912

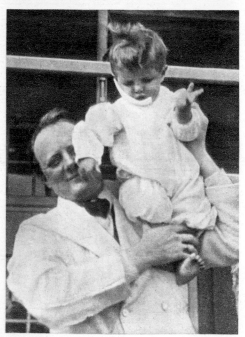

60 Mr Churchill with his mother, now Mrs George Cornwallis-West, at an Earl's Court exhibition commemorating the Armada. 29 July 1912

61 At Portsmouth with Mrs Churchill after launching the dreadnought battleship *Iron Duke*. 14 October 1912

62 Golfing with Maxine Elliott, the American actress, at Cannes. February 1913

63 He fails to keep his head down and foozles his drive. Mr Churchill had little aptitude for golf and so he abandoned it quite early in life. February 1913

64 On the Monte Carlo promenade with Millicent, Duchess of Sutherland.
1913

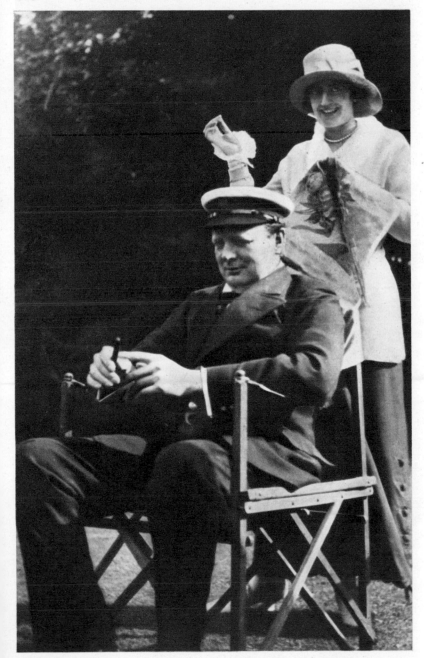

65 Staying with Mrs Churchill's cousins, Lord and Lady Stanley of Alderley.
6 September 1913

66 With Admiral Lord Fisher after a meeting of the Committee of Imperial Defence.
1913

67 With his friend, F. E. Smith, later Lord Birkenhead, Mr Churchill watches a review by naval recruits. 1913

68 With the Secretary of State for War, Colonel Seely, he attends a review of the Brigade of Guards. 1913

69 In his uniform of an Elder Brother of Trinity House, he leaves the Guildhall during the State visit of M Poincaré. 1913

70 Mr Churchill was an early flying enthusiast and introduced an Air Arm into the Navy. With Mrs Churchill he visits Hendon. 1914

71 He flew a great deal himself and often handled the controls though he never flew solo. He leaves his aircraft at the Central Flying School at Upavon on Salisbury Plain. 1914

72 Mr and Mrs Churchill holiday together on the beach at Sandwich shortly before the outbreak of the First World War. Twenty-five years later the outbreak of the Second World War found Mr Churchill again as First Lord of the Admiralty. July 1914

73 Walking across Horse Guards Parade with his former First Sea Lord, Prince Louis of Battenburg, who had recently been forced to resign his appointment as a result of public clamour against those of German origin and name. 1914

74 With the King at a military review in Hyde Park. November 1914

75 A family group taken at Admiralty House early in 1915. Mr Churchill and his brother, Major John Churchill, stand at either end of the sofa. In the middle is their mother, Lady Randolph Churchill, with Mrs Churchill and Lady Gwendeline Churchill on either side of her. The children from left to right are Diana, Sarah (lying on her mother's lap), Randolph, Peregrine and John. 1915

76 Walking away from Downing Street with Lord Lansdowne and Lord Curzon after the formation of Mr Asquith's Coalition Government. Mr Churchill had been forced to leave the Admiralty and is now Chancellor of the Duchy of Lancaster. May 1915

77 With Mr Arthur Balfour, later Earl Balfour, former leader of the Conservatives, who succeeded him at the Admiralty. In his youth, Mr Balfour had been a friend and associate of Lord Randolph Churchill in the Fourth Party. May 1915

78 Mr Churchill addresses a meeting at Enfield Munition Works. Mrs Churchill is on the left. 1915

79 When the Government decided to abandon the enterprise of forcing the Dardanelles, Mr Churchill resigned from the Government and joined the army in France. He visits General Fayolle at the Headquarters of the French 33 Corps. Third from the left is Captain Spears (now Major General Sir Louis Spears). In the Second World War, General Spears was responsible for bringing General de Gaulle to London after the fall of France and served as the Liaison Officer between him and the Prime Minister. 1915

80 Mr Churchill, with the rank of Lt Colonel, was given command of a battalion of the Royal Scots Fusiliers. His second-in-command was Major Sir Archibald Sinclair who was to become leader of the Liberal Party and Minister for Air in Mr Churchill's war-time Government. 1916

81 At the Guildhall he listens to Field Marshal Lord Kitchener, Secretary of State for War, making a recruiting speech. Lord Kitchener was drowned a few weeks later when the ship which was taking him to Russia struck a mine and was lost with all hands. May 1916

82 Walking through Parliament Square with Mr David Lloyd George who had now succeeded Mr Asquith as Prime Minister. 1916

83 With his wife and Admiral Hood at Lord's. 1916

84 With the Crown Prince of Sweden at a Hyde Park parade. 1917

85 In 1917, Mr Churchill rejoined Mr Lloyd George's Government as Minister of Munitions. On an official visit to France he is accompanied by his brother, Major John Churchill. 1917

86 The Minister of Munitions tours one of the many factories in the North of England.
8 October 1918

87 Afterwards he addresses the munition workers during the lunch hour in the factory yard.
8 October 1918

88 Watching the march past of the 47th Division on the occasion of the re-entry of the King of the Belgians into Lille after its liberation. Behind Mr Churchill are Millicent, Duchess of Sutherland and his Private Secretary, Mr Edward Marsh. In the left foreground is Lt Colonel Bernard Montgomery. This is the first known photograph of Mr Churchill and the Field Marshal together. 28 October 1918

89 Five of the leading members of Mr Lloyd George's Coalition Government in levee dress. From left to right are Sir Laming Worthington-Evans, Minister without portfolio, Mr Churchill, Minister of Munitions, Lord Birkenhead, Lord High Chancellor, Mr Lloyd George, Prime Minister, Mr Austen Chamberlain, Secretary of State for India, Lord Curzon, Lord President of the Council.

90 Talking with the Prince of Wales on the occasion of the luncheon at the House of Commons to three American airmen who had flown the Atlantic to Lisbon. 5 June 1919

91 Mr Churchill attends an investiture in Hyde Park with the Prince of Wales, General Pershing and Mr John W. Davis, the American Ambassador in London. 19 July 1919

92 On a visit to the British Army of Occupation with the Chief of the Imperial General Staff, Field Marshal Sir William Robertson (extreme left), he inspects a guard of honour outside Cologne Cathedral. 1919

93 On the same visit to Germany he inspects British women workers at Stadtwald, near Cologne. 1919

94 With his cousin, the Marquess of Londonderry, Mr Churchill leaves the War Office.
1919

95 At a public dinner with the American Ambassador, Mr John W. Davis and Mrs Davis.
1919

97 Mr and Mrs Churchill arrive at Buckingham Palace with their daughter Sarah, to watch the march past of the Guards. With them is the Hon Mrs Arthur Henley. 1919

98 Mr Churchill at the Trooping the Colour ceremony in Hyde Park. His two elder children, Diana and Randolph, are on his left. King George V is taking the salute. 5 June 1920

96 Mr Churchill says goodbye to Earl Grey of Fallodon, formerly Sir Edward Grey, who is leaving a London station for the north. 1919

99 Mr Churchill played polo regularly until he was more than 50. June 1921

100 After a game of polo at Roehampton. Early in life Mr Churchill dislocated his shoulder and he had to wear a strap around his right arm to prevent it recurring. His last game was in Malta in 1926. 12 March 1921

101 Mr Churchill at his mother's funeral at Bladon, near Blenheim. Beside him are his brother and his nephew John. 2 July 1921

102 As Colonial Secretary he summoned a conference in Cairo to settle the affairs of the Middle East. On his right is Sir Herbert Samuel, later Lord Samuel, High Commissioner in Palestine and Sir Percy Cox, High Commissioner in Mesopotamia, is on his left. Behind Mr Churchill to the right is Mr T. E. Lawrence 'of Arabia'. Also present are General Haldane and Sir Percy Radcliffe. 1921

103 With Mrs Churchill at the wedding of Princess Mary, King George V's daughter, to Lord Lascelles. 28 February 1922

104 He strides up the beach at Deauville after a bathe in the sea. August 1922

105 The General Election of 1922 coincided for Mr Churchill with an attack of appendicitis. He was only able to go to his constituency of Dundee for the last few days and was still so weak that he had to be carried. He was defeated by the prohibitionist, Mr Scrymgeour. Following behind Mrs Churchill on the right is his detective, Sergeant Thompson. October 1922

106 In the last days of Mr Lloyd George's Coalition Government there was an inner triumvirate in whom power was concentrated. In addition to Lloyd George, they were Lord Birkenhead, the Lord Chancellor, and Mr Churchill. Together they leave Downing Street. 1922

CHAPTER THREE

During the next sixteen years, Mr Churchill was in office for less than five, from 1924 to 1929, when he served as Chancellor of the Exchequer in Mr Baldwin's Conservative Government. He had a sharp disagreement in 1930 with the Conservative leader on the Party's Indian policy and this, coupled with his criticisms of the defence policy of the National Government, involved his exclusion from office for more than ten years. For the most part he spent his time at his new home at Chartwell in Kent, building walls, making lakes, painting pictures and writing books. This was for him a period of great literary activity. He completed the *World Crisis*, his history of the First World War, wrote his four-volume life of the Duke of Marlborough, and by the time war came in September 1939, had completed his first draft of his *History of the English Speaking Peoples*. In addition he wrote the story of his early life and published two volumes of essays as well as writing a great number of newspaper articles.

Mr Churchill's literary activities were not only an agreeable occupation and the means by which he earned his living: they in a very real sense prepared him for the task to which he was to be summoned in 1940. The writing of the *World Crisis* taught him much about the mistakes made by the Allies in the First World War. And the study of the life of his great ancestor, the Duke of Marlborough, matured his strategical thought and cast it in the mould of the Grand Alliance which he was to re-create more than 200 years later. Posterity may well decide that his reading and writing of history between the two

1923 - *September* 1939

wars proved of supreme value to the free world when it belatedly faced the greatest menace by which it had ever been confronted.

Even before Hitler had come to power Mr Churchill was pointing to the dangers ahead. In November 1932 he told the House of Commons:

'The removal of the just grievances of the vanquished ought to precede the disarmament of the victors. To bring about anything like equality of armaments [between the vanquished and the victor nations] if it were in our power to do so, which it happily is not, while those grievances remain unredressed, would be almost to appoint the day for another European war – to fix it as if it were a prize-fight. It would be far safer to reopen questions like those of the Dantzig Corridor and Transylvania, with all their delicacy and difficulty, in cold blood and in a calm atmosphere and while the victor nations still have ample superiority, than to wait and drift on, inch by inch and stage by stage, until once again vast combinations, equally matched, confront each other face to face.'

With all the varied activities depicted in the pages that follow he found time for a good deal of foreign travel including two journeys to the United States and Canada. These pages are a kaleidoscope of a part of his life in which, though he enjoyed little power, he gradually enhanced his influence throughout the free world and, at a time when many people thought his political life was finished, he was preparing himself for the much greater tasks that lay ahead.

107 Leaving the house in Leicester with Mrs Churchill during the General Election of 1923 when he was defeated at West Leicester. The national results of the Election were: Conservatives 258; Labour 191; and Liberal 159. 7 December 1923

108 In March 1924, Mr Churchill stood as Independent anti-Socialist candidate in the famous by-election in the Abbey Division of Westminster. Every committee room was manned by a Conservative MP. He dictates a speech to his secretary, Miss Fisher, in his Sussex Square home. 6 March 1924

109 Soho was part of this Westminster constituency and Mr Churchill canvasses in the open air market in Berwick Street. 18 March 1924

110 He tours the Abbey Division where he was defeated for the third time running, but this time by only 43 votes. 9 March 1924

111 Mr Churchill speaks over a primitive public address system during the General Election of October 1924 when he was Conservative candidate for the Epping Division. This time he was successful by a large majority. The results of the Election were: Conservatives 412; Labour 151; Liberal 40. 4 October 1924

112 After the Conservatives had gained this triumphant majority, to everyone's surprise, the Prime Minister, Mr Baldwin, invited the ex-Liberal Free Trader, Mr Churchill, to join his Government as Chancellor of the Exchequer. Mr Austen Chamberlain, the new Foreign Secretary, is on the left. November 1924

113 Mr Churchill drives himself to the House of Commons while Chancellor of the Exchequer.
1925

114 On his way to deliver his first Budget speech to the House of Commons, he leaves Downing Street with his proposals for a return to the gold standard in Mr Gladstone's famous despatch box. 29 April 1925

115 Mr Churchill was a member of the House of Commons polo team which defeated the House of Lords. With him after the match are Captain G. R. G. Shaw, Captain Euan Wallace and Captain the Honourable F. E. Guest, Mr Churchill's first cousin. 18 July 1925

116 Arriving at Hurlingham to watch the British Army play polo against an American team.
c 1925

117 Wearing a 'paddy' hat and carrying a shillelagh, the Chancellor of the Exchequer is driven through Belfast to the Ulster Hall in an Irish jaunting car during a students' rag.
c 1926

118 As Chancellor he negotiated the Debt Settlement with Italy. Sitting with him after the signing of the agreement are the Italian Ambassador, Signor Grandi, the Italian Finance Minister, Count Volpi, and Sir Otto Niemeyer. In the back row against the chimney-piece are Mr Churchill's Private Secretaries, Sir James Grigg, later Secretary of State for War in the Second World War, and Sir Edward Marsh. 27 January 1926

119 In the summer a General Strike threatened to paralyse the country. With Sir Philip Cunliffe-Lister, President of the Board of Trade, he arrives at 10 Downing Street to see the Prime Minister. 3 May 1926

120 After his bathe, he walks back across the sands of Deauville with the Duke of Sutherland.
1 August 1927

121 Swimming in the sea at Deauville during the holidays.
1 August 1927

122 He drinks from a flask of brandy while out hunting the wild boar with his friend the Duke of Westminster in the Forest of Eu in Normandy. 31 January 1927

123 Mr Churchill supervises the damming up of a stream while staying with the late Lord Richard Cavendish at Holker in Lancashire. August 1927

124 After the funeral of his old Liberal chief, the Earl of Oxford and Asquith, Mr Churchill leaves Westminster Abbey with his sister-in-law, Mrs Bertram Romilly. Just in front of him on the right are the Prime Minister, Mr Stanley Baldwin, and his wife. February 1928

125 Inspecting the seaplane *Calcutta* moored in the Thames near the House of Commons. 2 August 1928

126 He builds a wall in the grounds of Chartwell. Bricklaying has been for many years a favourite occupation of his leisure hours. 1928

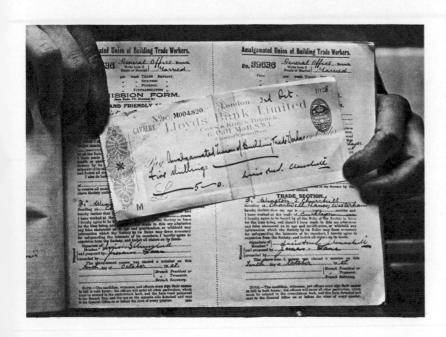

127 In October 1928 Mr Churchill joined the Amalgamated Union of Building Trade Workers. On the left is his application for membership and cheque for 5/-. His application was seconded by Mr James Lane, the Southern Counties Divisional Secretary. 10 October 1928

128 On the way to the House of Commons for his fifth and last Budget speech with his wife, daughter Sarah and son Randolph. Behind him in a top hat is his Parliamentary Secretary, Mr Robert Boothby, MP. 15 April 1929

129 With the Earl of Derby and the Duke of Westminster during an interval at the races at Aintree.

130 The General Election of May 1929 had brought the Labour Party into office once more. Mr Churchill says goodbye in a railway carriage at Victoria Station to his old friend and colleague Lord Birkenhead who is leaving for a visit to the United States. 19 July 1929

131 A fortnight later, Mr Churchill sails for Canada with his brother on a two months holiday. 3 August 1929

132 After touring Canada he arrived in California, where he stayed with Mrs Helen Russell. Here, at Pebble Beach, he paints a landscape.

133 In the Rockies, he stops to feed a chipmunk.

134 In Hollywood, he visits Mr Charles Chaplin at his film studio.

135 While in Los Angeles, he is the guest of honour at a luncheon given by Mr Louis B. Mayer, the head of the MGM film studios. On Mr Churchill's right is Mr William Randolph Hearst, the newspaper owner, and on his left, his host Mr Mayer. 18 September 1929

136 Ten days later Mr Churchill sailed on a yacht to the Island of Catalina where he caught a 188 lb Marlin Swordfish. 28 September 1929

137 On his return to the east coast of America, he pays a call on President Hoover at the White House in Washington. 9 October 1929

138 Back in England he entertains at Chartwell Governor Alfred Smith of New York, Hoover's unsuccessful opponent in 1928. 1930

139 Speaking at a Tory Rally at Cleve Court, the home of Lord Carson who is in the chair. 18 August 1930

140 Mr Churchill is one of the speakers at a meeting of the Indian Empire Society. Standing on the platform with him are Field Marshal Sir Claude Jacob and Lord Sumner. Seated behind him is Mr Buchan Hebburn, who is now Chief Conservative Whip. 11 December 1930

141 Mr Churchill is chaired through the streets of the city by the undergraduates after being installed by a popular vote as Lord Rector of Edinburgh University for the current year. 6 March 1931

142 Mr and Mrs Churchill entertain Mr Charles Chaplin at Chartwell. With them in the party are the Hon Tom Mitford, the second Earl of Birkenhead, who had succeeded his father in the previous year, Diana Churchill and Randolph Churchill. 19 September 1931

145 In front of the bathing cabins at Cap D'Antibes on the French Riviera, Mr Churchill settles down to paint a seascape. 1932

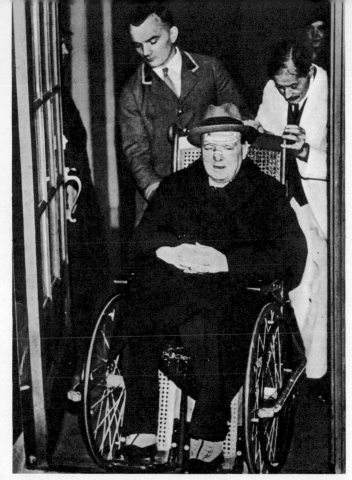

143 While in New York on a lecture tour, Mr Churchill was knocked down by a taxi as he was crossing Fifth Avenue to visit Mr Bernard M. Baruch. He leaves the hospital three weeks later. 31 December 1931

144 After his accident in New York he went to recuperate in Nassau in the Bahamas with his daughter Diana. The scar which he received on his forehead is still plainly visible. January 1932

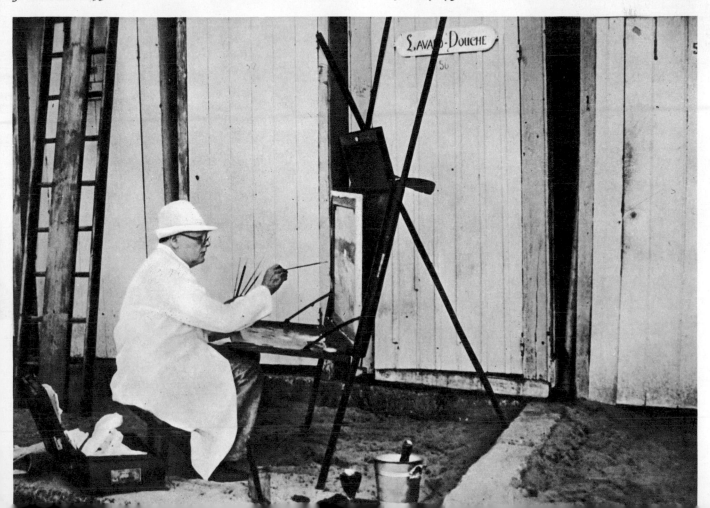

146 Staying with Lord Cranborne, now the Marquess of Salisbury, he sits with his wife and their daughter Sarah in the garden of Cranborne Manor. August 1932

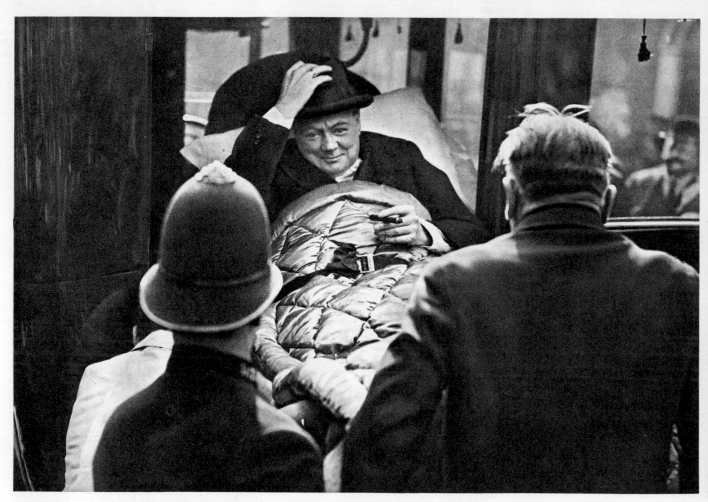

147 After a severe attack of paratyphoid, he leaves the nursing home tied to a stretcher on his way to recuperate at Chartwell. 10 October 1932

148 Mr and Mrs Churchill and their son Randolph go out hunting with the Duke of Westminster's boarhounds in Normandy.
20 January 1933

149 With Mr Lloyd George and Mr J. S. Elias, later Lord Southwood, the Chairman of Odhams Press, he attends a dinner in aid of the Printers Pension Fund. December 1934

150 He leaves his Committee Rooms during the hard-fought General Election of 1935. The Conservative Government was returned with a reduced but still substantial majority, but Mr Churchill himself was to remain out of office for another four years. 14 November 1935

151 King Edward VIII abdicated on 11 December 1936. The following day his brother King George VI was proclaimed King at an accession Council at St James's Palace. Mr Churchill is in the full dress uniform of an Elder Brother of Trinity House. By his side is Sir Herbert Samuel, the Liberal Leader. 12 December 1936

152 Three famous writers, Mr W. Somerset Maugham, Mr Churchill and Mr H. G. Wells in the garden of Mr Maugham's villa at Cap Ferrat on the French Riviera. April 1937

153 He christens a new LMS engine *Royal Naval Division* after the force he raised in 1914. The Division's commander, General Sir Ian Hamilton, stands by. 5 June 1937

154 Mr Churchill poses with one of the many exhibits of the 5th National Book Fair at Dorland Hall, Regent Street, London, which he has opened. 8 November 1937

155 Walking to the House of Commons from the Foreign Office with the Foreign Secretary, Lord Halifax, Mr Churchill discusses the situation caused by Hitler's annexation of Austria a week before. 29 March 1938

156 Walking away from Downing Street after conferring with the Prime Minister, Mr Chamberlain, during the Munich crisis. 10 September 1938

157, 158 Mr Churchill in his bricklaying clothes nails the tiles on the roof of a cottage which he had recently built at Chartwell. 1939

159 In his study at Chartwell. 8 March 1939

161 As Honorary Air Commodore of No 615 Auxiliary Squadron of the RAF, he flies with the Squadron which was stationed near Chartwell. 16 April 1939

162 He addresses a recruiting meeting in front of the Mansion House. 24 April 1939

160 7 April 1939 was Good Friday. Mussolini selected this date for his invasion of Albania. A week later an important foreign affairs debate took place in the House of Commons. Mr Churchill with Mr Brendan Bracken, MP leaves the latter's house in Lord North Street, Westminster, to speak in the debate. During the seven years before the war in which Mr Churchill warned Britain of the German danger and the need to rearm, Mr Brendan Bracken, now Viscount Bracken, was his staunchest Parliamentary supporter. 13 April 1939

163 In the garden at Chartwell during the visit of M Léon Blum.
10 May 1939

164 M Blum, the French Socialist leader, had come to England to try vainly to persuade the British Socialists to vote for conscription. Mr and Mrs Churchill entertained him at Chartwell. Beside Mrs Churchill, who is holding a tame fox cub, which had been caught at Chartwell, is Mr Richard Law, now Lord Coleraine, son of the former Conservative Prime Minister, Mr Bonar Law.
10 May 1939

165 War was now very near. On 14 July Mr Churchill was invited to an Anglo-French military parade in Paris. General Gamelin, the French C-in-C said to him: 'You have never seen the Rhine Sector. Come then in August. We will show you everything.' Accordingly Mr Churchill spent ten days in August as the guest of General Georges inspecting French defences. August 1939

166 Germany invaded Poland on 1 September. Britain mobilised immediately. The Prime Minister, Mr Chamberlain, asked Mr Churchill to visit him that afternoon and invited him to become a member of the War Cabinet. Mr Churchill leaves Downing Street after a talk with the Prime Minister. 1 September 1939

CHAPTER FOUR

Germany invaded Poland on 1 September 1939. Two days later, Britain and France declared war on Germany. The same day Mr Churchill joined the Government as First Lord of the Admiralty, the post he had occupied when the First World War had started in 1914. He had been out of office for eleven years.

In the first period of 'phoney war', or 'twilight war' as Mr Churchill called it, the Navy had far more to do than the Army or the Air Force. The Navy suffered some isolated reverses but on the whole all went well and the victory of the River Plate did much to sustain the morale of the nation during the first winter of the war.

Hitler's invasion of Norway in April 1940 gave the Western Allies a chance to get to grips with the enemy. Expeditions were sent to various parts of Norway, but nothing could compensate for the advantage Hitler had gained by his surprise tactics.

A vote of censure was directed against the Government; it was defeated, but the Government majority was far smaller than before. Mr Chamberlain tried to form a Coalition Government, but neither the Socialists nor the Liberals would serve under him. On May 10, he resigned and Mr Churchill was invited by the King to form a new administration. Mr Churchill has recorded:

'His Majesty received me most graciously and bade me sit down. He looked at me searchingly and quizzically for some moments, and then said: "I suppose you don't know why I have sent for you?" Adopting his mood, I replied: "Sir, I simply couldn't imagine why." He laughed and said: "I want to ask you to form a Government." I said I would certainly do so.'

The same day at dawn, the German armies began their invasion of the Low Countries. Seldom in history can anyone have been called to supreme power at a moment of such deadly peril. As Mr Churchill has written:

'Now at last the slowly-gathered, long-pent-up fury of the storm broke upon us. Four or five millions of men met each other in the first shock of the most merciless of all the wars of which record has been kept. Within a week the front in France, behind which

September 1939 - June 1942

we had been accustomed to dwell through the hard years of the former war and the opening phase of this, was to be irretrievably broken. Within three weeks the long-famed French Army was to collapse in rout and ruin, and our only British Army to be hurled into the sea with all its equipment lost. Within six weeks we were to find ourselves alone, almost disarmed, with triumphant Germany and Italy at our throats, with the whole of Europe open to Hitler's power, and Japan glowering on the other side of the globe.'

In the opening months of his administration, the new Prime Minister had to face a kaleidoscope of catastrophe and tragedy: the Battle of France, Dunkirk, the Bordeaux Armistice, the decision to attack the French fleet at Oran, the Battle of Britain and the entry of Italy into the war.

During the winter of 1940, Hitler abandoned his design of invading Britain. Instead, in the spring he fell upon Yugoslavia and Greece and in June 1941 attacked his ally Soviet Russia. In a broadcast speech that night, the Prime Minister said:

'No one has been a more consistent opponent of Communism than I have for the last twenty-five years. I will unsay no word that I have spoken about it. But all this fades away before the spectacle which is now unfolding. The past, with its crimes, its follies, and its tragedies, flashes away. I see the Russian soldiers standing on the threshold of their native land, guarding the fields which their fathers have tilled from time immemorial.'

While all this was going on, the Prime Minister was, by repeated letters and telegrams, establishing that personal friendship with President Roosevelt which was to be so serviceable to the Allied cause and which found its first important fruition when they met for the first of their numerous war-time conferences at Placentia Bay, in Newfoundland. Five more months were to pass before the Japanese attack on Pearl Harbour was to bring the United States into the war, but already with the signing of the Atlantic Charter and the Anglo-American Agreement on lend-lease, much had been achieved to bring aid from across the Atlantic.

168 In a broadcast speech which won him a wide measure of public confidence, he says: 'Here I am in the same post as I was in 25 years ago. Rough times lie ahead . . .' 1 October 1939

169 He visits Lord Gort, Commander-in-Chief of the British Expeditionary Force, at his French Headquarters. Reflected in the looking glass is Mr Churchill's aide-de-camp Commander C. R. Thompson who accompanied him on nearly all his war-time travels. 5 November 1939

167 On 3 September Great Britain declared war on Germany. The next day, Mr Churchill returns to the Admiralty as First Lord. The Board of Admiralty on hearing of his appointment has already signalled to the Fleet the laconic message 'Winston is back'. 4 September 1939

170 The First Lord seen at a full meeting of the Board of Admiralty. On the right of the First Lord sits the Financial Secretary, Mr Geoffrey Shakespeare, MP, and on his right, the First Sea Lord, Admiral Sir Dudley Pound. Behind the First Lord hangs a portrait of King William IV who as Duke of Clarence was Lord High Admiral from 1827–1828. The calendar records the date. 17 November 1939

171 The First Lord is cheered by the ship's company on board *HMS Exeter* which has just returned to Plymouth from the River Plate. A month before she had played a notable and heroic part in the destruction of the German pocket battleship *Graf Spee*. 15 February 1940

172 Inspecting British merchant seamen recently liberated from the German prison ship *Altmark* by the destroyer *Cossack* off the coast of Norway 'under the nose of the enemy and amid the tangles of one-sided neutrality' as Mr Churchill described it at the time. February 1940

173 On 10 May Hitler invaded the Low Countries. Mr Chamberlain resigned and Mr Churchill was called upon by the King to form a new Government. This famous portrait of the new Prime Minister was taken by Mr Cecil Beaton during the Battle of Britain.

174 The Cabinet Room at 10 Downing Street is also the private office in which the Prime Minister transacts most of his business.

175 10 Downing Street through the archway of the Foreign Office.

176 The emergency bedroom set aside for the Prime Minister under his flat in nearby Storey's Gate where he lived after Downing Street had been hit by a bomb and had been pronounced unsafe.

177 Invasion of Great Britain was now expected daily. After an inspection of coastal defences in Kent, the Prime Minister confers in Dover Castle with Admiral Sir Bertram Ramsay who was then Flag officer commanding Dover. 28 August 1940

178 Mr and Mrs Churchill visit the London docks by launch to inspect the damage caused in the great fire blitz. August 1940

179 Amid the ruined homes and factories of East London, the Prime Minister asks: 'Are we downhearted?' On his right is his detective escort, Sergeant Thompson. December 1940

180 With General Sikorski, the Prime Minister of Free Poland, and Commander-in-Chief of the Polish Army, Mr Churchill acknowledges the cheers of Polish soldiers stationed in Scotland. January 1941

181 On the same visit to Scotland, he reads *The Times* at a wayside station while his train is being shunted. 18 January 1941

182 Mr Chamberlain remained in Mr Churchill's Government as Lord President of the Council until his death on 9 November 1940. Five days later the Prime Minister leaves 10 Downing Street to attend his funeral. 14 November 1940

183 The Prime Minister visits the dockyard at Thurso and addresses the dockyard workers and sailors on board a warship. 18 January 1941

184 Mr Churchill signs the agreement by which Great Britain leases her Atlantic bases to the United States for 99 years in return for fifty over-age destroyers. On his right is Mr John Winant and on his left is Mr Vincent Massey, Canadian High Commissioner. 27 March 1941

185 Dressed in his academic robes as Chancellor of the University, Mr Churchill presents honorary degrees to Mr Menzies, the Australian Prime Minister and Mr Winant, the United States Ambassador, at Bristol. 12 April 1941

186 He speaks in a Liverpool shipyard and thanks seamen and dockers for the part they are playing in fighting in the Battle of the Atlantic. 25 April 1941

187 About this time President Roosevelt sent Mr Averell Harriman to London as his special representative. The Prime Minister shows him around a naval establishment in Plymouth which had been badly bombed; hence the steel helmets worn by the dockyard workers at their machines. 2 May 1941

188 The Prime Minister, the Chancellor of the Exchequer, Sir Kingsley Wood, and the Minister of Aircraft Production, Lord Beaverbrook, attend the jubilee luncheon of the *News of the World* at the Dorchester Hotel. Before the war, Mr Churchill had been a frequent contributor to the columns of that paper. 1 May 1941

189 He tries out a Sten gun at an armament establishment. Behind him in a bowler hat is Captain Margesson, Secretary of State for War. On the right of the picture are his two constant companions on his trips, Commander Thompson RN and Sergeant Thompson CID. 17 June 1941

190 A few minutes later he inspects the results of his shooting. Sir Archibald Sinclair, Secretary of State for Air, and Lord Cherwell, the Prime Minister's scientific and statistical adviser, join the group round the target. 17 June 1941

191 The Prime Minister and Mr Brendan Bracken, Minister of Information, inspect the ruins of the House of Commons which had been destroyed by bombs the previous night. For the rest of the war the Commons met in Church House or the House of Lords. 11 May 1941

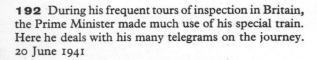

AGE 66

192 During his frequent tours of inspection in Britain, the Prime Minister made much use of his special train. Here he deals with his many telegrams on the journey. 20 June 1941

193 The Prime Minister carries his steel helmet and respirator at an inspection of London Civil Defence personnel in Hyde Park. On his right is Mr Herbert Morrison, Minister of Home Security. On his left is Admiral Sir Edward Evans (Evans of the *Broke*), London Regional Commissioner for Civil Defence. Behind him is Mrs Churchill. 14 July 1941

194 After his review of the Civil Defence Services he speaks at a luncheon in the County Hall. He ends with the words:

'We do not expect to hit without being hit back, and we intend with every week that passes to hit harder. Prepare yourselves, then, my friends and comrades in the Battle of London, for this renewal of your exertions.' 14 July 1941

195 In the middle of 1941, the Prime Minister crosses the Atlantic in *HMS Prince of Wales* for his famous meeting with President Roosevelt in Placentia Bay, off the coast of Newfoundland. During the voyage he confers with Admiral Sir Dudley Pound, First Sea Lord, General Sir John Dill, Chief of the Imperial General Staff, and Air Chief Marshal Sir Wilfred Freeman, Vice-Chief of the Air Staff. July 1941

196 Blackie, the ship's cat of *HMS Prince of Wales*, breaks ranks and the Prime Minister touches it for luck. August 1941

197 At Divine Service on board ship. Behind the Prime Minister and the President are the British and American Chiefs of Staff. 'I chose the hymns myself,' he has recorded, '*For those in Peril on the Sea* and *Onward, Christian Soldiers*. Every word seemed to stir the heart. It was a great hour to live.' 10 August 1941

198 He takes a walk on the deck of the *Prince of Wales* with his friend and colleague Lord Beaverbrook who had just flown out from England to join the conference. 11 August 1941

199 The Prime Minister's talks with the American President culminated in the proclamation of the Atlantic Charter. Immediately after the signing of the Charter, they are joined by Admirals King and Leahy. Behind them to the right is Mr Averell Harriman. 14 August 1941

200 On his voyage back from Placentia Bay, the Prime Minister visited Iceland, already occupied by American troops. He salutes the Stars and Stripes and the flag of the American Marines. Behind him is Ensign Franklin D. Roosevelt, third son of the President. August 1941

201 Back in England, he acknowledges the farewell cheers of the crew of *HMS Prince of Wales*. Less than four months later on 10 December this brand-new battleship was to sink with nearly all her crew off Malaya after an attack by Japanese torpedo bombers. 19 August 1941

202 The Canadian Prime Minister, Mr Mackenzie King, walks with Mr Churchill in the garden at Chequers, the official country residence of all British Prime Ministers. August 1941

203 Shortly after his return from the United States, the Prime Minister visits the sandbagged Ministry of Information in London University, and in the presence of the Minister, Mr Brendan Bracken, he gives the first of his innumerable and famous 'V' signs. August 1941

204 The War Cabinet in the garden of 10 Downing Street. In the front with Mr Churchill are Sir John Anderson, the Labour Party leader Mr Attlee, and Mr Eden. Behind are the two other Labour members, Mr Greenwood and Mr Bevin, next to Lord Beaverbrook and Sir Kingsley Wood. 16 October 1941

205 The Defence Committee are photographed on the same day. In the front row with the Prime Minister are Lord Beaverbrook, Mr Attlee, Mr Eden and Mr A. V. Alexander. Standing behind are Air Chief Marshal Sir Charles Portal, Admiral Sir Dudley Pound, the Liberal Party leader Sir A. Sinclair, Captain Margesson, General Dill, General Ismay and Colonel Hollis. 16 October 1941

206 The Prime Minister shakes hands with King George VI after Their Majesties have had luncheon with him at 10 Downing St. 28 October 1941

207 On 7 December the Japanese struck at Pearl Harbour. Within a few days the Prime Minister sailed for the United States. His daughter Mary sees him off. December 1941

208 The Prime Minister landed at Hampton Roads and flew to Washington where he is met by President Roosevelt who drives him to the White House for their second war-time meeting. 22 December 1941

209 He parades the lawn of the White House in his siren suit for the benefit of a battery of American newsreel photographers. December 1941

210 On Boxing Day the Prime Minister for the first time in his life addresses a joint session of the Congress of the United States. Behind him on the Senate rostrum sit Representative William P. Cole Jnr, the temporary Speaker of the House of Representatives and Vice-President Henry Wallace. On his right is Senator Alben Barkley.

'I cannot help reflecting that if my father had been American and my mother British, instead of the other way round,' says Mr Churchill, 'I might have got here on my own. In that case, this would not have been the first time you would have heard my voice. In that case I should not have needed an invitation, but if I had, it is hardly likely it would have been unanimous.' 26 December 1941

211 Mr Harry Hopkins's daughter, Diana, carries the President's Scottie, Fala, into the White House garden to see Mr Churchill. December 1941

212 From Washington the Prime Minister flew to Ottawa to address the Canadian House of Commons. At his press conference he is presented with a 'wedge' hat of sealskin fur to add to the many he has acquired on his travels. 31 December 1941

213 Speaking to Canadian MPs in Ottawa, he recalls how during the fall of France some French generals had predicted that Britain would 'have her neck wrung like a chicken' within three weeks. 'Some chicken, some neck', comments the Prime Minister. 31 December 1941

214 On his return journey to Britain, the Prime Minister flies from Virginia to Bermuda and takes over the controls for a time. 14 January 1942

215 A twenty-year pact of mutual aid was signed between the Soviet Union and Britain. On the terrace at Downing Street with the Soviet Ambassador, M Maisky, the Foreign Minister, M Molotov, Mr Attlee, Mr Lyttelton, Mr Eden and Sir Alexander Cadogan. 26 May 1942

AGE **67**

216 June found the Prime Minister back in the United States for the first meeting of the Pacific War Council. Accompanied by Brigadier William C. Lee, Commandant of Fort Jackson, he watches the climax of large scale paratroop manoeuvres. 26 June 1942

CHAPTER FIVE

In this chapter, which covers the last three years of the Second World War, the Prime Minister is incessantly on his travels around the World concerting the alliance and plans which were to bring utter defeat to the Axis powers. In August 1942 he set off on what was his longest and perhaps his most important mission. After flying to Cairo where he reorganised the Middle East Command and appointed Generals Alexander and Montgomery to lead the British forces in the forthcoming Battle of Alamein, he flew on to Moscow for his first meeting with Stalin. It had been decided that it was impossible to open a second front in France in 1942 and the Prime Minister thought it right to break this unwelcome news to Stalin in person. Though this news was ill received, the Prime Minister was able to telegraph to the President after his week in Moscow:

'I am sure that the disappointing news I brought could not have been imparted except by me personally without leading to really serious drifting apart. It was my duty to go. Now they know the worst, and having made their protest are entirely friendly . . .'

At the beginning of November came the brilliant victory of the 8th Army at Alamein, in the Western Desert. Of this battle the Prime Minister later wrote: 'Before Alamein we never had a victory. After Alamein we never had a defeat.' Alamein was swiftly followed by the joint Anglo-American descent on the coast of French North Africa. These twin victories led to the junction of the two Allied armies and made necessary the meeting of the Prime Minister and the President at Casablanca in January 1943, the conference where the policy of unconditional surrender was proclaimed.

Only three months after Casablanca the Prime Minister conferred again with the President in Washington. Here plans were made for the invasion of Italy and, looking further ahead, to the organisation of the United Nations when victory was won. On this

August 1942 - August 1945

visit the Prime Minister addressed the United States Congress for the second time. Here he was able to give a favourable account of the fighting in Africa:

'The African excursions of the two dictators have cost their countries in killed and captured 950,000 soldiers . . . . Arrived at this milestone in the war, we can say, "One continent redeemed".'

A thousand dramatic events crowd into these three tremendous years. This summary and the pictures can do no more than seize upon the highlights. Hard upon the liberation of Africa came the invasion of Sicily, the fall of Mussolini and the invasion of Italy. Meanwhile ceaseless planning proceeded for the invasion of France and conferences were held at Quebec, Washington, Cairo and, in November 1943, at Teheran. At this last, the 'Big Three' met for the first time.

All this culminated in the Normandy landings in June 1944. August finds Mr Churchill in Rome; September in Quebec once more; and in October he flies off to Moscow for the second time for another conference with Stalin. On Christmas Day 1944, he flew to Athens for one of his most dramatic personal interventions in the war; this prevented Greece falling under Communist tyranny. Meanwhile, Hitler was making his final desperate effort with the Rundstedt offensive in the Ardennes.

The New Year opens with the doom-laden three-power conference at Yalta. Within a few weeks the Allies are across the Rhine and on 8 May 1945 Germany surrenders. Mr Churchill's Coalition Government breaks up, an election is held and while the Potsdam Conference is in session the overwhelming victory of the Socialists is announced. 'It may well be a blessing in disguise' remarked Mrs Churchill. 'At the moment it seems quite effectively disguised' was Mr Churchill's retort.

217 Within a few weeks of his return, the Prime Minister flew to Cairo to reorganise the Middle East Command. In the garden of the British Embassy he sits with the South African Prime Minister, Field Marshal Smuts. They had fought on opposite sides in the Boer War but became firm friends in the First World War. 8 August 1942

218 In Moscow for his first meeting with Marshal Stalin. At the airport Mr Churchill is greeted by the Commandant of the City, accompanied by Marshal Shaposhnikov, Chief of the Soviet General Staff, and M Molotov. 17 August 1942

219 The first photograph ever taken of Mr Churchill and Marshal Stalin together. It was sent by radio, hence its inferior quality. Also in the picture is Mr Averell Harriman, President Roosevelt's special representative. August 1942

220 The Prime Minister tests the radio-telephone in one of the first Churchill tanks to be delivered to the British Eighth Army in the desert. August 1942

221 On his way back to Britain, Mr Churchill stopped for further talks in Cairo where the Army High Command had now been reconstituted. While in Egypt he visits the forward lines in the Western Desert with General Alexander and General Sir Alan Brooke. 22 August 1942

222 While the Prime Minister was away in the Middle East, Mrs Churchill visits an exhibition of recent war photographs. 20 August 1942

223 British and American troops had landed in North Africa in November 1942. In mid-January 1943 the President and the Prime Minister met at Casablanca for their fourth conference of the war. At its conclusion, an attempt was made to reconcile the two quarrelling French Generals, Giraud and De Gaulle. With some difficulty they are persuaded to pose together for the photographers. 24 January 1943

224 At the conclusion of the Casablanca talks, the President and the Prime Minister hold an open air press conference. 24 January 1943

225 From Casablanca the Prime Minister flew to Tripoli where he spent a night with General Montgomery in his very well-camouflaged caravan headquarters near Castel Benito. 7 February 1943

226 The next day in Tripoli they drive through the streets after reviewing the victorious Eighth Army. In the back of the car is Lt General Sir Oliver Leese, the GOC, 30 Corps. 8 February 1943

227 In May, the Prime Minister sailed to the United States for his fifth conference with the President and his second speech to Congress. Off Staten Island he disembarks from the *Queen Mary*. Behind him on the stairway is Admiral Andrews of the US Navy. 11 May 1943

228 Mr Churchill reaffirms his support for the President's policy of unconditional surrender. Behind him on the dais sits the Vice-President of the United States, Mr Henry Wallace, and the Speaker of the House, Mr Sam Rayburn. On the platform are Representative Sol Bloom, Representative Joseph Martin, Senator A. W. Barkley, Senator Charles L. McNary and Senator Tom Connolly. 19 May 1943

229 From the United States the Prime Minister flew direct to North Africa. He visits the Headquarters of the British First Army. Photographing the Prime Minister in the centre is Major John Profumo, now a junior Minister in Sir Winston's Government. 1 June 1943

230 At General Eisenhower's head-quarters in Algiers the Prime Minister dis-cusses the plans for the invasion of Italy. Around him gather Mr Eden, General Sir Alan Brooke, Air Chief Marshal Tedder, Admiral Sir Andrew B. Cunningham, General Alexander, General Marshall, Gen-eral Eisenhower and General Montgomery. 4 June 1943

231 Back in London he received the Freedom of the City. Driving with him to the Guildhall ceremony in a horse-drawn landau are Mrs Churchill and their daughter Mary. 30 June 1943

232 Six weeks later he arrived in Quebec for a conference with Mr Mackenzie King, the Prime Minister of Canada. Mr Churchill welcomes President Roosevelt who joined them in Canada. 16 August 1943

233 A week later at the end of the conference, the British and Canadian Prime Ministers drive through the streets. With them is Mr Churchill's bodyguard, Sgt Thompson. 23 August 1943

234 At Harvard University he received an honorary degree of Doctor of Law. In his speech he moots the idea of common citizenship for the inhabitants of Great Britain and the United States. 6 September 1943

235 The Prime Minister returned from his American trip on *HMS Renown*. At sea with his wife and daughter Mary, he watches a destroyer coming alongside with despatches. September 1943

236 En route in *HMS Renown* for the Cairo Conference with President Roosevelt, he stops in Malta where he inspects the dockyard with the Governor, Field Marshal Lord Gort. November 1943

237 In Cairo he has talks with Generalissimo Chiang Kai Shek and Madame Chiang as well as President Roosevelt. Also at the conference are the Chinese Generals, Chang Chen and Ling Wei, the American Generals, Somervell, Stilwell and Arnold, and the senior British officers, Field Marshal Sir John Dill, Admiral Lord Louis Mountbatten and Major General Carton de Wiart, VC. 27 November 1943

238 The first meeting of the Teheran Conference was held at the Soviet Embassy. Behind the 'Big Three' on the Embassy terrace are Mr Harry Hopkins, M Molotov, Mr Averell Harriman, the Prime Minister's daughter Sarah and Mr Eden. 28 November 1943

239 With Mr Eden beside him he reads the citation before presenting the Sword of Stalingrad to Marshal Stalin as a tribute from King George VI and the people of Britain to its defenders. 29 November 1943

240 When the conference is over, the photographers of many countries crowd in en masse up the steps of the Soviet Embassy.

241 Mr Churchill's 69th birthday fell during the three-power conference. He celebrates it with a dinner at the British Legation for the American and Soviet leaders. 30 November 1943

242 The 4th Hussars had provided the guard for the Cairo Conference. Stopping for a few days in Cairo on the return journey, he inspects his old regiment as its Colonel-in-Chief. December 1943

243 His trip interrupted by a severe attack of pneumonia he spent several days in bed at General Eisenhower's villa near Carthage. He entertains General Eisenhower and General Alexander to a Christmas Day luncheon party. 25 December 1943

244 Mrs Churchill had flown out to the General's villa at Carthage when the Prime Minister was ill. Shortly after their return from Africa, she accompanies her daughters Mary and Sarah to the House of Commons to hear the Prime Minister speak. 18 January 1944

245 A new American carbine had arrived in Britain. General Eisenhower, Mr Churchill and General Omar Bradley test it for themselves at an American camp. March 1944

246 Flanked by General Smuts, Mr Mackenzie King, and the Prime Ministers of Australia and New Zealand, he signs an agreement for closer Commonwealth solidarity. 16 May 1944

247 On 6 June the Allied armies landed in Normandy. On D Day plus 6 he tours the beachhead with General Montgomery. 12 June 1944

249 Major General Cecil Moore, Chief Engineer of the US Army in Europe, takes Mr Churchill round the devastated but free port of Cherbourg. June 1944

248 A few days later he visits General Eisenhower in Normandy. June 1944

250 The attack by flying bombs has started. The Prime Minister watches an anti-aircraft battery which is deployed between London and the coast. 30 June 1944

251 In a forward observation post Mr Churchill watches a British Army artillery shoot near Florence. 20 August 1944

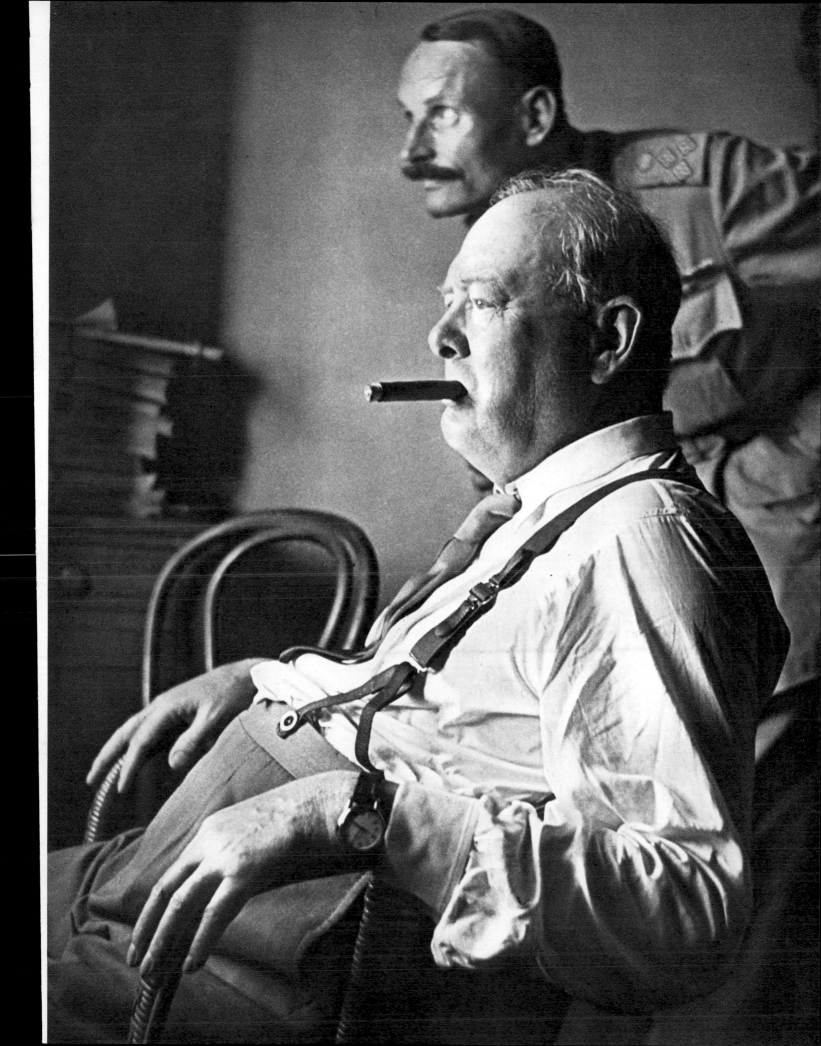

252 While visiting the Allied armies in Italy the Prime Minister meets Marshal Tito, the legendary leader of the Communist partisans in Yugoslavia, at Caserta, near Naples. 12 August 1944

253 Ten days later at the British Embassy in Rome, he entertains the Italian Crown Prince Umberto who became Regent after the abdication of his father King Victor Emmanuel. 23 August 1944

254 General George Marshall, Admiral William Leahy with the President and the Prime Minister on the terrace of the Citadel during the Quebec Conference where plans were made for the war in the Far East. 17 September 1944

255 At the airport on his second visit to Moscow, with Marshal Stalin and M Molotov. Behind are M Maisky and M Vishinsky. October 1944

256 Mrs Churchill is waiting for her husband at the airport when he returns from his visit to Russia. 22 October 1944

257 Paris was liberated by American and French forces on 23 August 1944. On 11 November the Prime Minister visits Paris and walks with General de Gaulle from the Arc de Triomphe down the Champs Elysées. Behind the Prime Minister are the British Ambassador, Mr Duff Cooper, Mr Anthony Eden and M Georges Bidault, Foreign Minister in the provisional de Gaulle Government. 11 November 1944

258 With General de Gaulle and General de Lattre de Tassigny the Prime Minister inspects units of the French army at Besançon. 30 November 1944

259 On Christmas Day the Prime Minister flew to Athens where civil war had broken out. He leaves the cruiser *HMS Ajax* which was his Headquarters during his visit. Behind him is his doctor, Sir Charles Wilson, later Lord Moran. With papers in his hand is one of his Private Secretaries, Mr John Colville. 30 December 1944

260 He leaves the British Embassy in Athens with the Greek Regent, Archbishop Damaskinos. The civilian is Mr Osbert Lancaster, the author and pocket cartoonist. 30 December 1944

261 Early in the New Year he went to Malta where he had talks with President Roosevelt. From Malta, the President and the Prime Minister flew to the Crimea for the Three-Power Conference with the Russians at Yalta. During a rare interlude, even the Russian interpreter Pavlov hazards a smile. February 1945

262 The President and the Prime Minister stay on behind for a private talk at the conference table. February 1945

263 Outside the Livadia Palace where the Yalta talks were held.
February 1945

264 On the way back from the Yalta Conference, the Prime Minister entertains King Ibn Saud of Saudi Arabia in the Fayoum Oasis some 40 miles from Cairo. February 1945

265 Visiting the Rhine Front in an armoured car Mr Churchill passes through the ruined town of Xanten. 24 March 1945

267 General Simpson shows the Prime Minister around a captured section of the Siegfried Line. March 1945

268 By the riverside he stops for a picnic luncheon with Generals Brooke and Montgomery. 26 March 1945

266 Mr Churchill crosses the Rhine with General Simpson, General Sir Alan Brooke and General Montgomery. 25 March 1945

269 The King's First Minister appears on the balcony at Buckingham Palace together with the King and Queen and the two princesses on the afternoon of VE Day. This photograph, signed by the Royal Family, hangs in Sir Winston's bedroom at Chartwell. 8 May 1945

270 Broadcasting from 10 Downing Street he concludes with the words: 'Long live the cause of freedom. God save the King.' 8 May 1945

271 A close-up of King George VI and the Prime Minister on the balcony of Buckingham Palace on VE Day. 8 May 1945

272 From Buckingham Palace he returns to the Ministry of Health where standing between Mr Attlee and Mr Ernest Bevin he addresses the crowd of 50,000 assembled in Whitehall:

    'This is your victory. Victory in the cause of freedom in every land. In all our long history we have never seen a greater day than this. Everyone has done their bit. Everyone has tried. Neither the long years, nor the dangers, nor the fierce attacks of the enemy, have in any way weakened the resolve of the British nation. God bless you all.'

8 May 1945

274 A fortnight later, the Labour and Liberal Parties resigned from the war-time Coalition. The Prime Minister is leaving for Buckingham Palace to tender his resignation to the King. He was invited to form a new 'caretaker' Government.

23 May 1945

273 In the course of the afternoon he found time to pay calls on the United States, Soviet and French Ambassadors. With his daughter Mary he toasts the Allied victory over Germany at the Soviet Embassy with the Soviet Ambassador and Madame Gusev. 8 May 1945

275 Parliament was dissolved on 15 June and a General Election was announced. The Prime Minister in the course of his thousand mile tour of Britain picnics by the roadside between Birmingham and Coventry, with his daughter Sarah. 25 June 1945

276 The final meeting of his election campaign is held at the Walthamstow Stadium. The hat in his hand is borrowed. 3 July 1945

277 Polling took place on 5 July 1945 but votes could not be counted until three weeks later. Mr and Mrs Churchill take a brief holiday at Hendaye near Biarritz as the guests of General Brudenau. July 1945

278 Visiting the ruins of the German Chancellery in Berlin during the Potsdam Conference. 16 July 1945

279 Outside the Conference Hall in Potsdam, with Marshal Stalin and Mr Truman who succeeded to the Presidency on 12 April 1945 after the death of President Roosevelt. Mr Churchill too was soon to be replaced by his war-time Cabinet colleague Mr Attlee. July 1945

280 A session during the Potsdam Conference. On Marshal Stalin's right are M Molotov and M Vishinsky; on his left is the Russian interpreter Pavlov. 19 July 1945

281 The defeat of the Conservative Government was announced on 26 July. Mr Churchill resigned. His belongings are moved from 10 Downing Street. 1 August 1945

CHAPTER SIX

This chapter covers the six years from the fall of Mr Churchill's predominantly Conservative 'caretaker' Government in the summer of 1945 to his return to office at the General Election of October 1951. Though he was no longer at the head of affairs, these six years were full of work and activity. Throughout the period, Mr Churchill was Leader of the Opposition and of the Conservative Party. In his latter capacity he devoted much time to concerting the plans which in the General Election of February 1950 slashed the Socialist majority to six, and which eighteen months later restored the Tory Party to power.

During these years he also travelled widely, particularly in Europe where he launched his great campaign for a United Europe. This campaign culminated in the closing months of 1954 in the nine-power London Agreement which commits both Britain and Germany to a long term participation in the defence of Western Europe. Amidst all this activity, Mr Churchill found time to write his six monumental volumes of war memoirs.

Perhaps the most notable speech he made in this period was that at Fulton, Missouri, entitled 'The Sinews of Peace'. In this historic pronouncement, he spoke of the iron curtain which the Russians had rung down between Eastern and Western Europe, of the police states which have been erected and of the menace which Russian communism constitutes to the peace and freedom of the world; and he called for a fraternal association of the English speaking peoples under the Charter of the United Nations to ward off the peril.

Public opinion, still largely the victim of war-time propaganda which had suggested

August 1945 - October 1951

that Russia was one of the peace-loving democracies, was ill prepared for these warnings and the Fulton speech was widely condemned both in Britain and the United States. Once again, as in the thirties, Mr Churchill found himself alone in sounding the 'alert'. This time, however, the democracies were not so wilfully complacent for so long. Within three years, the warnings of Fulton had been accepted as common ground throughout the West and some of the necessary measures had been taken, of which the signing of the North Atlantic Treaty in March 1949 was the most considerable.

The first intimation of Mr Churchill's European campaign was given at Metz on Bastille Day 1946. This was followed two months later by a notable contribution on the same theme at Zurich University. Early in 1947 the European Movement was formed. This led to the Congress of Europe at The Hague in May of the following year and in due course to the establishment of the Council of Europe in Strasbourg. His leadership of the United Europe Movement must be considered his greatest contribution to the building of peace and security while in Opposition.

Mr Churchill had to lay his paint box aside during the war and he only painted one small picture at Marrakesh just after the Casablanca Conference. Freed in 1945 from the daily routine of government, he took his paints with him wherever he travelled and this chapter includes a number of pictures of him at his easel in different parts of the world.

In these early post-war years, Mr Churchill, like his father before him, also found time, as the pictures show, for a new hobby – racing.

282 On the day of the Japanese surrender the House of Commons adjourned to render thanks. Mr Churchill is now Leader of the Opposition and Mr Attlee is Prime Minister. With them are their deputies, Mr Eden and Mr Morrison. 15 August 1945

283 At the first reunion in the Albert Hall of the officers and men who fought at Alamein, the great British victory over Rommel in the desert in November 1942. Sitting next to him is Field Marshal Viscount Montgomery of Alamein. 23 October 1945

285 Repudiated by the electors at home, Mr Churchill is still popular in liberated Europe. Here he drives through Brussels. 16 November 1945

284 With Mrs Churchill he attends a local celebration of a national thanksgiving day at Westerham near his home at Chartwell. 10 November 1945

286 Leaving their new home in Hyde Park Gate for a holiday in Miami. 9 January 1946

287 The world no longer at war, if only in uneasy peace, he takes to his paint box once more at the Surf Club in Miami. 2 February 1946

288 But the main purpose of his visit to the United States was to sound a warning against Russian Communist aspirations at Fulton, Missouri, on the occasion of his becoming a Doctor of Law. He said:
'A shadow has fallen upon the scenes so lately lighted by the Allied victory. . . . From Stettin in the Baltic to Trieste in the Adriatic, an iron curtain has descended across the Continent.'
5 March 1946

289 It had been the President's wish that Mr Douglas Chandor should paint a portrait of the 'Big Three'. As a preliminary, Chandor decided to paint them each separately. Mr Churchill was the second to be painted. But Stalin never consented to sit. 19 March 1946

290 Accompanied by Mrs Churchill and Mrs Roosevelt, he lays a wreath on the President's grave at his home in Hyde Park. 16 March 1946

291 With Mr Attlee he attends a Memorial Service for Field Marshal Lord Gort, Commander of the BEF in France in 1940. 10 April 1946

292 At the invitation of Queen Wilhelmina of the Netherlands, who is seated between them on the barge, Mr and Mrs Churchill visit Amsterdam. While in the Netherlands, the Queen and the Dutch Government presented him with the 613 letters which his ancestor, John, Duke of Marlborough wrote to the Grand Pensionary (the ancient title of the First Minister) during the ten years of the Grand Alliance against Louis XIV. 10 May 1946

293 While awaiting the Victory Parade in London, Mr Churchill talks with the Canadian Prime Minister, Mr Mackenzie King. On the left is Mr Attlee, and on the extreme right Field Marshal Smuts of South Africa. 8 June 1946

294 On Bastille Day, Mr Churchill visited Metz, the capital of the eastern French province of Lorraine, with M Robert Schuman, French Minister of Finance. In a perceptive and inspiring speech he said: 'The first word I give you here today is *Europe*.' 14 July 1946

295 He receives the Freedom of the City of Luxembourg. 15 July 1946

296 He inspects the Guard of Honour after his installation at Dover Castle as Lord Warden of the Cinque Ports. 14 August 1946

297 'I am now going to say something that will astonish you,' he says in a speech at Zurich. 'The first step in the re-creation of the European family must be a partnership between France and Germany. In this way only can France recover the moral leadership of Europe. There can be no revival of Europe without a spiritually great Germany. The structure of the United States of Europe, if well and truly built, will be such as to make the material strength of a single state less important. Small nations will count as much as large ones and gain their honour by their contribution.' 19 September 1946

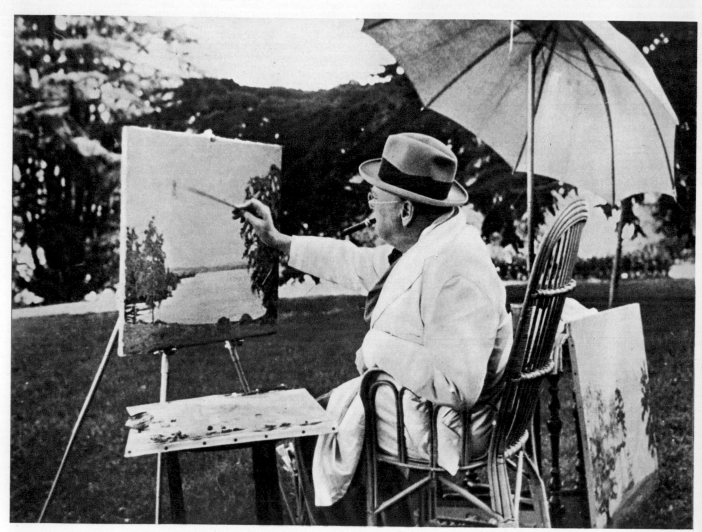

298 Mr Churchill painting at the Swiss villa on the shores of the Lake of Geneva where he spent a holiday this summer. 7 October 1946

299 The unity of Europe continues to be his main theme. Here he visits Berne in Switzerland and listens to an address of welcome. 17 September 1946

300 With the French Prime Minister, M Paul Ramadier, he inspects the Moroccan Spahis who form part of the military parade in the courtyard of the Invalides when he is presented with the Médaille Militaire, the highest of French military decorations. 10 May 1947

301 The French Prime Minister had himself been awarded the Médaille Militaire while serving as a sergeant in the First War.
10 May 1947

302 Speaking in the Albert Hall at a meeting to launch the European Movement, he says: 'We hope to reach again a Europe purged of the slavery of ancient days in which men will be as proud to say "I am a European" as once they were to say "Civis Romanus sum".' 14 May 1947

303 He addresses a vast audience at a Conservative West Country rally in the grounds of Blenheim. 4 August 1947

304 Two days earlier at nearby Woodstock, the oldest Royal Borough in the country where his father Lord Randolph Churchill was first elected to Parliament in 1874, he received the Freedom of the Borough from the Duchess of Marlborough who was Mayor. 2 August 1947

305 At the London Zoo in Regent's Park he feeds his lion Rota which had been presented to him during the war. 'The assistant secretary . . . was a charming man, highly competent, but physically on the small side,' he has recorded in his *War Memoirs*. 'Indulging in chaff, I now showed him a magnificent photograph of Rota with his mouth open, saying, "If there are any shortcomings in your work I shall send you to him. Meat is very short now." He took a serious view of this remark. He reported to the office that I was in a delirium.'
10 September 1947

306 While at the zoo, he also feeds the albino kangaroo Digger presented by Australian stockowners.
10 September 1947

307 Speaking in the Dome at Brighton at the end of the Conservative annual conference with Lord Woolton in the chair. 'I do not envy the man, whoever he is, who has to face the problems of British survival in the next few years,' said Mr Churchill. 'But I am sure that his power to help the nation in its dire need would be crippled, if not destroyed, if he were committed beforehand to a programme of pledges and promises which he would be no more able to redeem than the unfortunate Mr Attlee and Mr Morrison.'

4 October 1947

308 Playing gin rummy with Viscount Camrose while flying back to England from a holiday at Marrakesh. Lord Camrose, who died in 1954, was proprietor of the *Daily Telegraph* and one of his closest friends. In the background is Mr Churchill's doctor, Lord Moran. 19 March 1948

309 At the end of the historic Congress of Europe at The Hague, Mr Churchill is deeply moved by the ovation which he receives after the speech in which he said:
'But if we all pull together and pool the luck and the comradeship – and we shall need all the comradeship and not a little luck if we are to move together in this way – and firmly grasp the larger hopes of humanity, then it may be that we shall move into a happier sunlit age, when all the little children who are now growing up in this tormented world may find themselves not the victors nor the vanquished in the fleeting triumphs of one country over another in the bloody turmoil of destructive war, but the heirs of all the treasures of the past and the masters of all the science, the abundance and the glories of the future.'
On the platform with him are Dr Kerstens (Holland), M Paul Ramadier (France), Dr Retinger (Secretary General of the Congress) and Mr Denis de Rougemont 7 May 1948

310 After the christening of his fifth grandchild, Arthur Nicholas Winston Soames, the eldest of the four children of Mr and Mrs Christopher Soames. 28 March 1948

311 King Haakon of Norway greets Mr and Mrs Churchill on their arrival by air in Oslo as his guests. 11 May 1948

312 Mr Churchill unveiling the memorial in Westminster
Abbey to the officers and ratings of the submarine branch of
the Navy who lost their lives in the Second World War, and
also all ranks of the Commandos and Airborne forces. On the
right is one of the three bronze figures – a submarine rating on
the lookout. After the unveiling ceremony, he made a brief
speech which he concluded with these words:

'Of them and in presence of their memorial, we may repeat
as their requiem as it was their theme and as the spur for
for those who follow in their footsteps, the well-known
lines:

Heard are the voices.
Heard are the sages
The worlds and the ages.
Choose well; your choice is
Brief and yet endless.
Here eyes do regard you
In Eternity's stillness.
Here is all fullness
You brave to reward you.
Work and despair not.'

21 May 1948

313 Arriving with his daughter Diana and his poodle,
Rufus, at Euston Station on his way to the Tory Conference.
8 October 1948

314 Two days before his 74th birthday, Mr Churchill goes
hunting near Chartwell with the Old Surrey and Burstow Hunt
28 November 1948

315 From the deck of the Cunard liner *Queen Elizabeth* he acknowledges the cheers of the waiting crowd. 24 March 1949

316 With Mr Henry R. Luce, proprietor of *Time*, *Life* and *Fortune*, at a dinner given by him at the Ritz Carlton. 25 March 1949

317 On the platform with Mr Bernard Baruch at the mid-century convocation of the Massachusetts Institute of Technology in Boston. He said: 'Is time on our side? This is not a question that can be answered except within strict limits. We have certainly not an unlimited period of time before a settlement should be achieved. The utmost vigilance should be practised but I do not think myself that violent or precipitate action should be taken now. War is not inevitable. The Germans have a wise saying, "The trees do not grow up to the sky." '
31 March 1949

318 With an uncharacteristically Baldwinian sealed-lips gesture he ducks a question at a press conference on board the *Queen Mary* just before sailing home to England. 2 April 1949

319 Watching a new tractor clearing undergrowth at one of the Chartwell farms. Squatting on the ground is Mr Anthony Eden; standing by the tractor is Mr Christopher Soames who at that time was managing the farms. Summer 1949

320 Walking in the garden at Chartwell with Mr Bernard M. Baruch.
11 July 1949

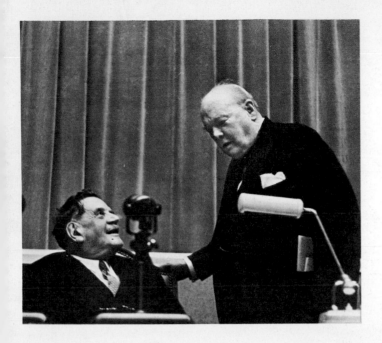

322, 323 The work of the European movement bore fruit, and in August 1949 the Council of Europe held its first meeting in Strasbourg. Nearly all the leading statesmen of Europe were gathered together. Here Mr Churchill talks with M Edouard Herriot of the French delegation and below with M Spaak of Belgium, who then presided. 12 August 1949

321 British and Italian plain clothes men try to ensure privacy for him while he paints at Madreno on Lake Garda in North Italy. 27 July 1949

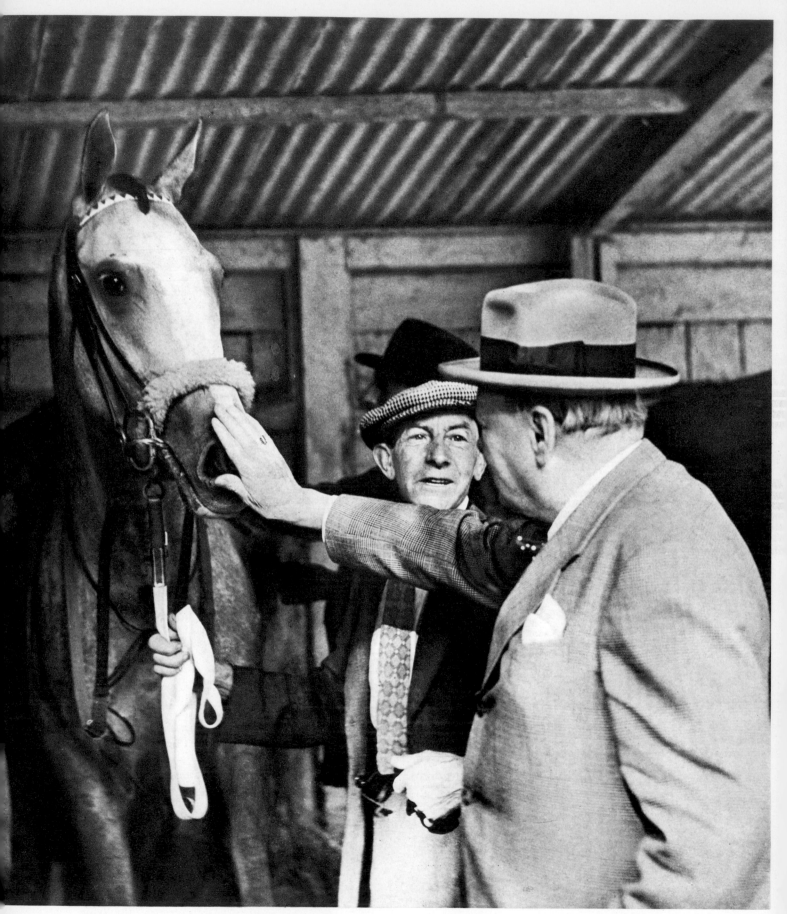

324 After the war Mr Churchill took up racing as his father Lord Randolph Churchill had previously done when out of office. Lord Randolph won the Oaks with his filly Abbesse de Jouarre which the British racing public promptly called the 'Abscess on the Jaw'. Mr Churchill had 'beginner's luck' and his first horse Colonist II, seen here, won thirteen races with a total of £11,938 in stakes. 10 September 1949

325 He watches Colonist II winning the Lime Tree Stakes.
10 September 1949

326 Congratulating Colonist II two years later when he won the Winston Churchill Stakes at Hurst Park. This race which was worth £1,777 15s., was established after the war in honour of Mr Churchill.

327 In the New Year he took a holiday in Madeira where he is favoured by sunshine and he resumes his painting. January 1950

328 He interrupted his holiday and flew home to England in a specially chartered flying boat. On arrival he says: 'I heard there was going to be a General Election so I thought I had better come back in case I was wanted.' 12 January 1950

329 During the campaign he visited Devonport to speak for his son, Randolph Churchill, who was the unsuccessful Conservative candidate. With his son and daughter-in-law, he is on his way to a meeting. February 1950

330 Outside the Conservative Club in Wanstead during a tour of his constituents on Election Day. The bulldog named Token belongs to one of Mr Churchill's supporters, Mrs Sewell. The results were: Labour 315 seats; Conservative 296 seats; Liberal 10 seats. 23 February 1950

332 Driving through the streets of Copenhagen on a three-day visit to Denmark when he was made a Doctor of Philosophy. 'As life unfolds I have been astonished to find how many more degrees I have received than I have passed examinations,' he said in returning thanks. 'I was never very good at those. But now I am treated as if I were a learned man. This is a good argument for not being discouraged by the failures or shortcomings of youth but to persevere and go on trying to learn all your life.' 10 October 1950

333 At the Empress Hall with Mrs Churchill and Field Marshal Montgomery during the fifth Alamein reunion. 20 October 1950

334 With the Prime Minister, Mr Attlee, he greets the King and Queen as they arrive to open the Festival of Britain. 4 May 1951

331 A study of Mr Churchill as he sits in the garden of Chartwell piercing a cigar. 1950

AGE **76**

335 Mr and Mrs Churchill and Mr and Mrs Christopher Soames, in a launch on the Grand Canal in Venice. 23 August 1951

336 Mr and Mrs Churchill photographed with some of their family on the Pink Terrace at Chartwell. To the left of the hammock are Mr and Mrs Duncan Sandys; sitting cross-legged is their eldest son, Julian. On Mr Churchill's knee is Emma Soames; her elder brother Nicholas is sitting on the cushion. Between Mr and Mrs Churchill is their grandson, Winston, and their granddaughter Arabella is at the end of the hammock on the right. Standing beside Arabella on the right is her father Mr Randolph Churchill. 1951

337 At the window of the Conservative Headquarters in his constituency of South Woodford during the General Election. 6 October 1951

338 Mr Churchill visits Plymouth again to speak in support of his son, Randolph, who was again unsuccessfully fighting Devonport Division. With his father and grandfather on the platform is Mr Randolph Churchill's son, Winston. 23 October 1951

339 Visiting the constituency of Mr Attlee, Walthamstow, to speak for the unsuccessful Conservative candidate. 24 October 1951

340 Outside the South Kensington polling station after recording his vote for the successful Conservative candidate for the constituency in which he then lived. The national result of the election was a narrow victory for the Tories: Conservative 321 seats; Labour 294 seats; Liberal 6 seats. The next day, Mr Churchill became Prime Minister of Great Britain again at the age of 76. 25 October 1951

CHAPTER SEVEN

The General Election ended six years of Socialist rule. Mr Churchill found himself once more back at Downing Street with the small majority of 19. In his new Government, Mr Anthony Eden returned to the Foreign Office where he had served during the last four years of the war, Mr R. A. Butler became Chancellor of the Exchequer, Field Marshal Alexander, Minister of Defence and Mr Harold Macmillan, Minister of Housing. Other leading members of the new administration were: Sir David Maxwell Fyfe, Home Secretary; Lord Woolton, Lord President of the Council; and Lord Salisbury, Lord Privy Seal.

The new Government found the country on the verge of an economic precipice. The balance of trade was set against us and the Bank of England's gold and dollar reserves were melting away week by week. In his Election speeches, Mr Churchill had asked the electorate for three years in which to put things right. This chapter covers these three years and concludes with the celebration of his eightieth birthday.

Looking back, Sir Winston, as he had by then become, could feel that in the main he had achieved the task which was entrusted to him. Trade was booming, unemployment was negligible, gold and dollars were once more flowing into the Bank of England instead of out of it; and the goal of 300,000 new houses a year, which had been so much derided by the Government's opponents, had been rapidly reached and passed.

Other work included the unscrambling and return to private enterprise of the steel industry which the Socialists had nationalised, the freeing of road transport from State

October 1951 - November 1954

ownership and the progressive abandonment of controls and rationing. At the end of the three-year period, the only commodity which was still rationed was newsprint. These solid achievements plainly met with the approbation of the public, and during the last six months of 1954, by-election results showed a steady swing of opinion towards the Government which, at the end of three years of office, and in spite of its small majority, appeared to be still firmly in the saddle.

On the whole, things had also gone well abroad. The war in Korea was ended and an armistice had been negotiated in Indo-China. A united Europe was still to be achieved, but great progress was made in the face of ever changing difficulties and at the end of 1954 British leadership promoted a settlement which made possible German re-armament within a European framework.

Throughout these three years, Sir Winston did his utmost, as always, to encourage and procure good feeling and a close unity of policy between Britain and the United States. In these three crowded years, he visited Washington three times – in January 1952, January 1953 and June 1954. In addition, he attended the three-power conference in Bermuda in December 1953 with President Eisenhower and M Laniel, the French Prime Minister.

So as this picture story, extending over eighty years, comes to its close, we see Sir Winston still in harness and still leading as vigorous and varied a life as these pages have depicted throughout.

341 Back once more at Downing Street, one of his earliest visitors is the West German Chancellor, Doctor Konrad Adenauer. 4 December 1951

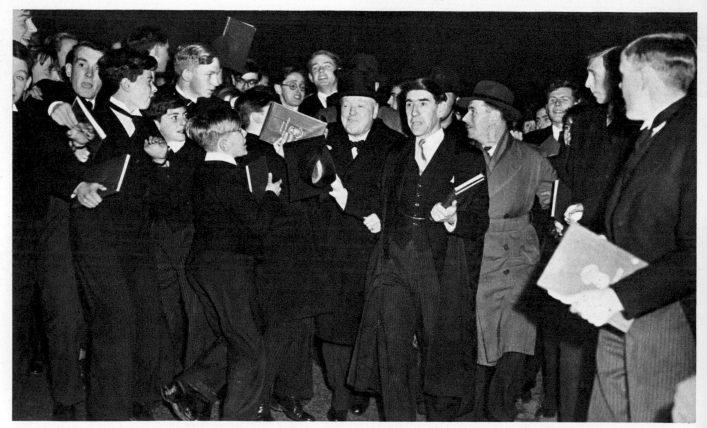

342 For a number of years, Mr Churchill made a habit of visiting his old school, Harrow, to sing the old school songs with the boys. After the singing he walks with the Headmaster, Mr R. W. Moore, from the Great Speech Room to the Headmaster's house. 7 December 1951

343 A few days later, Mr Churchill and Mr Eden went to Paris for talks with the French Prime Minister, M Pleven, and the French Foreign Minister, M Robert Schuman. The night ferry train is stopped at Sevenoaks so that Mr Churchill can join Mr Eden on board. 16 December 1951

344 The end of the year found Mr Churchill and Mr Eden bound for Washington for talks with President Truman and Mr Dean Acheson. The American Ambassador in London, Mr Walter Gifford, visits them on board the *Queen Mary* at Southampton before they sail. 31 December 1951

AGE **77**

345 From New York, Mr Churchill flew to Washington. Mr Truman escorts him into Blair House where Mr Churchill stayed during his visit. 5 January 1952

346 The visitors cruise down the Potomac with the President and Mr Acheson in the presidential yacht. 5 January 1952

347 From Washington, the Prime Minister proceeded to Ottawa. At a State dinner in the Canadian capital, he says:

'Peace does not sit untroubled in her vineyard . . . . All can see for themselves the strange clouds that move and gather on the horizon . . . . But this time at least we are united from the beginning . . . . We shall provide against and thus prevail over the dangers and the problems of the future . . . withhold no sacrifice, grudge no toil, seek no sordid gain, fear no foe.'

14 January 1952

348 Back in Washington, he is invested with the Eagle and Diploma of the Society of Cincinnatus which is limited to direct male descendants of officers who served three years in the Army and Navy during the American Revolutionary War. Mr Churchill's claim to membership derives from his great-great-grandfather, Lt Reuben Murray, who served with the 17th Connecticut Regiment and the 7th Albany Regiment in the New York Militia. 16 January 1952

350 On 6 February, King George VI died. The new Queen and the Duke of Edinburgh were at the time in Kenya. They flew home immediately. Waiting to meet Her Majesty at London airport with Mr Churchill are Mr Attlee, Leader of Her Majesty's Opposition, Sir David Maxwell Fyfe, Home Secretary, Mr Clement Davies, the Liberal Leader, and Mr Anthony Eden, Foreign Secretary. 7 February 1952

349 The following day, he addresses a joint session of Congress. Seated behind him is the Vice-President, Mr Alben Barkley. 17 January 1952

351 In August, Mr Anthony Eden married the Prime Minister's niece, Miss Clarissa Churchill. The reception was held at Downing Street where the bride and groom talk with Mr and Mrs Churchill. 14 August 1952

352 At the christening of his 8th grandchild, Jeremy Bernard Soames, son of Mr and Mrs Christopher Soames. The child was named Bernard after his godfather, Field Marshal Viscount Montgomery of Alamein who is holding the hand of Nicholas Soames. Mrs Churchill is talking with Emma Soames. 17 August 1952

353 A study for the cover of *Picture Post.*
October 1952

354 The Queen with seven Commonwealth Prime Ministers and two Finance Ministers. From left to right are: Mr D. S. Senanayake (Ceylon), Sir Godfrey Huggins (Rhodesia), Mr Holland (New Zealand), Mr Churchill, Mr St Laurent (Canada), Mr Havenga (South Africa), Mr Khawaja Nazimuddin (Pakistan) and Sir Chintamen Deshmukh (India). 4 December 1952

355 Staying for a few days in New York, he talks in Mr Bernard Baruch's apartment with the Republican president-elect, General Eisenhower. January 1953

356 A few days later, the Prime Minister travelled once more to Washington. He pins a flower in Mr Truman's buttonhole at a dinner given in honour of the retiring President at the British Embassy. 8 January 1953

359 In March Marshal Tito of Yugoslavia came to London for talks with the British Government. Marshal Tito, who travelled by sea and landed in London at Westminster Pier, is welcomed by the Prime Minister and the Foreign Secretary, Mr Anthony Eden. 16 March 1953

357 Kissing his new godchild, the daughter of his Private Secretary, Mr John Colville, at her christening. 11 February 1953

358 In bleak March weather he goes to the races at Sandown Park to see his horse Non-Stop run. 13 March 1953

360 Sir Winston and Lady Churchill leaving Buckingham Palace for the Coronation. Sir Winston, who was made a Knight of the Garter on 24 April, wears his uniform of Warden of the Cinque Ports. 2 June 1953

361 In the Abbey Sir Winston brings up the rear of the procession of Commonwealth Prime Ministers. 2 June 1953

362 Driving through Trafalgar Square after the Coronation with a mounted escort from his old regiment, the 4th Hussars. 2 June 1953

363 Three generations of Churchills at Downing Street after the Coronation. Below Sir Winston's belt hangs the Great George which was originally presented to John, Duke of Marlborough by Queen Anne and later by George IV to the Duke of Wellington. Sir Winston's son, Randolph, was a Gold Staff officer in the Abbey, and his grandson, Winston, was page to Viscount Portal. 2 June 1953

Photograph by Toni Frissell

364 At a garden party at Blenheim Palace for overseas visitors, he greets the Oni of Ife, ruler of three million subjects in Nigeria. 7 June 1953

365 As an Elder Brother, he boards the Trinity House yacht *Patricia* at the Coronation review at Spithead. 15 June 1953

366 He greets the Italian Prime Minister, Signor Alcide De Gasperi, on the steps outside 10 Downing Street. 23 June 1953

368 Leaving Downing Street with his dog Rufus for his home at Chartwell. 10 August 1953

367 On August Bank Holiday at Chequers he sits admiring the rose garden.
3 August 1953

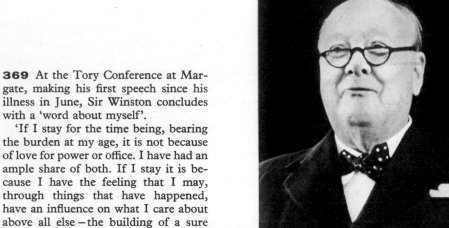

369 At the Tory Conference at Margate, making his first speech since his illness in June, Sir Winston concludes with a 'word about myself'.

'If I stay for the time being, bearing the burden at my age, it is not because of love for power or office. I have had an ample share of both. If I stay it is because I have the feeling that I may, through things that have happened, have an influence on what I care about above all else – the building of a sure and lasting peace. . . .'

11 October 1953

370 Guest of honour at the Lord Mayor's banquet. In the chair is the newly elected Lord Mayor, Sir Noel Vansittart Bowater. Sir Winston is wearing his Garter Star and Sash, and around his neck is the Order of Merit.

9 November 1953

371 In December, the Prime Minister, President Eisenhower and M Laniel, the French Prime Minister, met in Bermuda. The Prime Minister awaits the arrival of M Laniel at Kindley airport. 3 December 1953

372 Leaving the conference room in Bermuda with the President. M Laniel is standing on the left. 5 December 1953

373 During his absence in America, Lady Churchill flew to Stockholm where in the Concert Hall, on behalf of Sir Winston, she receives the Nobel Prize for Literature for 1953 from King Gustav. 12 December 1953

374 On his way to greet the Queen. She is arriving in the Solent on the *Britannia* on her return with the Duke of Edinburgh from their Commonwealth tour. 14 May 1954

375 Sir Winston spent the night on board the Royal yacht but disembarked at Tower Bridge so as to be present with Her Majesty's Ministers at Westminster Pier to greet the Queen. Hat in hand, the Prime Minister shakes HRH Prince Charles by the hand. 15 May 1954

376 At the Albert Hall he addresses a mass meeting of Conservative women. 27 May 1954

AGE **79**

378 Accompanied by Mr Eden, Sir Winston flew to Washington for a week-end conference with President Eisenhower. He waves goodbye to the crowd at London airport. 24 June 1954

379 He is greeted by the President and Mrs Eisenhower and by Mr John Foster Dulles, Secretary of State, on his arrival at the White House to talk over 'a few family matters'. 25 June 1954

380 Three days later in brilliant sunshine the four statesmen sit talking together in the garden of the White House. 28 June 1954

377 On his way to be installed as a Knight of the Garter at a service held in St George's Chapel, Windsor. As the latest joined member of the Order, Sir Winston leads his brother Knights from the Castle, where Her Majesty has invested him with the Insignia. 14 June 1954

381 He is driven through the streets of Ottawa after meeting the Canadian Prime Minister, Mr St Laurent. 1 July 1954

382 He holds open the car door for the French Prime Minister, M Mendès-France, after a luncheon at Chartwell. 23 August 1954

383 The United States Secretary of State, Mr John Foster Dulles, shakes hands with the Prime Minister and Mr Eden after lunching with them at Downing Street. 17 September 1954

384 Mr Eden calls for three cheers for Sir Winston at the Conservative Conference at Blackpool. Standing behind are Mrs Duncan Sandys and Mr Christopher Soames. 10 October 1954

385 Another distinguished visitor for the Prime Minister is His Imperial Majesty Haile Selassie I, the Emperor of Ethiopia.
22 October 1954

387 Graham Sutherland's portrait of Sir Winston is presented to him by the members of both Houses of Parliament in the Westminster Hall. Among those behind him are Sir Anthony Eden; Mrs Attlee; Lord Kilmuir; the Speaker, Mr Morrison; and Mr Attlee. 30 November 1954

388 On the evening of his 80th birthday, Sir Winston receives an enthusiastic ovation from the great crowds who have been waiting outside 10 Downing Street all day to see him. 30 November 1954

386 In his Chancellor's robes, a few days before his 80th birthday, Sir Winston speaks to the members of Bristol University. 26 November 1954

INDEX

ACKNOWLEDGMENTS

The editors are grateful to the following for the loan of photographs: to Aerofilms Ltd for 6; Associated Newspapers Ltd for 129, 141; Associated Press Ltd for 148, 165, 208, 210, 212, 233, 275, 283, 284, 294, 295, 297, 300, 302, 303, 307, 313, 318, 323, 326, 327, 333, 335, 340, 343, 347, 348, 360, 361, 366, 370, 371, 376; Barratt's Photo Press Ltd for 40, 41, 43, 109, 176, 352, 375; Mr Cecil Beaton for 173; Camera Press Ltd for 216, 279, 351 and photograph on jacket; Central Office of Information for 363; Central Press Photos Ltd for 7, 70, 96, 106, 160, 204, 231, 246, 276, 287, 305, 320, 387, 388; Courier and Advertiser, People's Journal, Dundee for 105; Daily Herald for 17, 110, 111, 130, 149, 281, 359; Daily Mail for 55, 67, 77; Daily Mirror Picture Service for 16, 36, 37, 49, 61; Mr William Gordon Davis for 102, 144; Miss Gertrude Ellis for 12; Fox Photos Ltd for 153, 161, 163, 166, 168, 172, 182, 222, 271, 293, 298, 373, 383; Toni Frissell for frontispiece and 365; Mr Helmut Gernsheim for 174, 175; Gernsheim Collection for 2, 4, 5, 9, 26, 74, 99; Graphic Photo Union for 191, 301, 304, 330, 338; Illustrated for 159; Imperial War Museum for 10, 25, 71, 79, 88, 92, 169, 177, 178, 180, 181, 183, 184, 185, 186, 187, 192, 195, 196, 197, 199, 200, 201, 207, 209, 213, 214, 215, 217, 218, 220, 221, 223, 224, 225, 226, 227, 228, 229, 230, 232, 234, 235, 236, 237, 239, 241, 242, 243, 247, 249, 250, 251, 252, 253, 254, 256, 257, 258, 259, 261, 262, 263, 264, 265, 266, 268, 270, 272, 273, 278, 280; International News Photos for 288, 311, 312, 315, 317, 319, 339, 350, 357, 358, 374, 381, 382; Kemsley Picture Service for 8, 13, 156, 170, 203, 379; Keystone Press Agency Ltd for 112, 126, 145, 165, 179, 219, 240, 245, 248, 267, 274, 282, 286, 289, 290, 299, 314, 321, 324, 325, 332, 334, 337, 349, 354, 368, 378, 389; Life Magazine for 316, 331; London News Agency Photos Ltd for 76, 100, 104, 113, 116, 120; Manchester Guardian for 42; Northcliffe Newspapers Group Ltd for 377; P.A.-Reuter Photos Ltd for 39, 44, 47, 50, 60, 66, 69, 78, 81, 83, 90, 91, 94, 95, 97, 98, 108, 115, 118, 136, 142, 147, 291, 310, 328, 344, 345, 380; Pictorial Press for 238, 255, 285; Picture Post Library for 14, 15, 18, 21, 27, 34, 38, 45, 46, 51, 52, 53, 54, 62, 64, 86, 87, 93, 103, 117, 157, 158, 308, 309, 322, 355; Planet News Ltd for 82, 140, 143, 150, 164, 167, 206, 260, 277, 329, 367, 385, 386, 390; Press Portrait Bureau for 89; Sport and General Press Agency Ltd for 48, 68, 72, 84, 107, 193; The Times for 124, 205, 364; Topical Press Agency Ltd for 63, 73, 85, 119, 121, 122, 125, 127, 128, 131, 137, 139, 151, 154, 155, 162, 171, 189, 190, 194, 211, 269, 296, 306, 336, 346, 353, 356, 362, 372, 384; United Press News Pictures for 244.

The following photographs are from private sources: 1, 3, 11, 19, 20, 22, 28, 29, 30, 31, 32, 33, 35, 56, 57, 58, 59, 65, 75, 80, 101, 123, 132, 133, 134, 135, 138, 146, 152, 188, 198, 202, 369.

The editors also wish to thank the following librarians for the special facilities which they provided: Mr G. H. Brenes of the Central Office of Information; Mr J. H. Castleton of the Daily Herald; Mr Charge, Mr Mitchenall and Mr White of the Imperial War Museum; Mr Martin Prince of Keystone Press Agency; Mr Aldis of the Daily Mail; Mr Pryor of the News Chronicle; Mr Saville of Kemsley Picture Service; and Miss Jessy of 'Life' Library.